HIGH TIDE
and an
EAST WIND

Ungava Bay

Tinker Harbour

Baie Johan Beetz

Newfoundland

Grand Codroy River

Quebec

St. Lawrence R.

New Brunswick

N.S.

St. John Estuary

Me

N.S.

Merrymeeting Bay

Vt NH

Mass.

Ct

Cape Cod

Long Island Sound

New York

Pennsylvania

Md

N.J.

Cape May

W. Va.

Virginia

North Carolina

Cape Hatteras

South Carolina

Black Duck
Topography

HIGH TIDE
and an
EAST WIND
The Story of the Black Duck

BRUCE S. WRIGHT
Northeastern Wildlife Station,
Fredericton, New Brunswick

Line Drawings
by Peter Ward
Courtesy of the
Frederic C. Walcott Memorial Fund
of the
North American Wildlife Foundation

STACKPOLE
BOOKS
Lanham • Boulder • New York • London

with the

WILDLIFE MANAGEMENT INSTITUTE
Washington, D. C.

Published by Stackpole Books
An imprint of The Rowman & Littlefield Publishing Group, Inc.
4501 Forbes Boulevard, Suite 200, Lanham, Maryland 20706
www.rowman.com

Unit A, Whitacre Mews, 26-34 Stannary Street, London SE11 4AB

Distributed by NATIONAL BOOK NETWORK

Copyright © 1954 by the Wildlife Management Institute Washington, D.C.
First Edition
Reissued Stackpole Books cloth edition 2017

ISBN 978-0-8117-3723-4 (cloth)
ISBN 978-0-8117-6675-3 (electronic)

Foreword

Scientific study of the behavior of ducks on the breeding grounds in the Canadian prairies was undertaken by the Delta Waterfowl Research Station in Manitoba more than a decade ago. That was the first attempt on this continent to go into the basic breeding ecology of the ducks of the west, and since that time, much valuable management data have been accumulated.

Prior to 1945, no such effort had been made to study the breeding ecology of the ducks breeding in eastern Canada, the main source of the waterfowl of the Atlantic Flyway. In that year, Bruce S. Wright was engaged by Ducks Unlimited to undertake a study of the breeding ecology of the Black Duck, an assignment which developed into the present Northeastern Wildlife Station. The work of this station, which is operated by the Wildlife Management Institute, is supported by numerous cooperators including Ducks Unlimited, Canadian Industries, Ltd., the University of New Brunswick, New Brunswick Department of Lands and Mines, U. S. Fish and Wildlife Service, Canadian Wildlife Service, and National Research Council of Canada.

The study of the Black Duck has been a major project of this Station, and during the past nine years, Mr. Wright and his associates have followed Black Ducks from Florida to Ungava Bay, and from Lake Manitoba to the bleak shores of the Avalon Pensinsula of Newfoundland. This manuscript, the result of these studies, should furnish basic information upon which a sound management program can be based. It should be of particular interest to all wildfowlers and wildlife workers in the Atlantic Flyway.

Ira N. Gabrielson

President, Wildlife Management Institute

Acknowledgments

So many people contributed to the advancement of this study that it is impossible to mention all of them by name. Without their help the project never would have been completed, and I gratefully acknowledge my debt to all. Certain ones, however, have made major contributions, and they must be mentioned. The first is the late Aldo Leopold, Professor of Wildlife Management at the University of Wisconsin. It was under his masterful hand that the study assumed its final form, and his advice was invaluable at all times.

H. Albert Hochbaum, Director of the Delta Waterfowl Research Station at Delta, Manitoba, helped materially in the early part of the study, and critically read the final manuscript.

Howard L. Mendall, the Leader of the Maine cooperative Wildlife Research Unit at the University of Maine, assisted with fieldnotes and laboratory identifications of duck foods.

Dr. A. C. Martin of the U. S. Fish & Wildlife Service worked up the stomach contents of ducks collected in Ungava Bay.

B. W. Cartwright, Chief Naturalist of Ducks Unlimited, contributed data from the western breeding grounds.

Milton B. Trautman, Research Associate of the Franz Theodore Stone Laboratory at Put-in-Bay, Ohio, contributed some original data on pairing of Black Ducks.

William H. Carrick of Toronto, Ontario, contributed many fine photographs.

Peter Ward of the Delta Waterfowl Research Station prepared the line drawings.

Brian C. Carter, the Station Biologist of the Northeastern Wildlife Station, was present for all but the first year of the study and collected and compiled voluminous fieldnotes.

Dr. A. Lucas of the Department of English, University of New Brunswick, read the manuscript.

These men made major contributions to the success of the study, and they have my sincere thanks.

Table of Contents

List of Plates

xi

Preface

There appear to be two fairly distinct populations of the Black Duck. The first is the northeastern population, which is essentially maritime, nesting from New England to Ungava Bay and wintering on the northern half of the Atlantic seaboard. The second and largest is the western population, nesting in the area drained by the Great Lakes and James Bay and wintering on the southern half of the Atlantic seaboard and in the Mississippi valley and the Gulf coast.

Although the first population is the smaller of the two, it is in this northeastern region that the Black Duck reaches the peak of its importance. Here it is outstanding as the number one game duck of the flyway, but in the other regions it is mixed with all the ducks from the prairie breeding grounds and consequently diminishes in importance. It is proper, therefore, that this work should pay more attention to the northeastern population than to the western. The detail of the breeding ecology was gathered in the northeast, but data from all parts of the range are included in the other sections.

Introduction

The Canvasback has been called the "gold standard" of the central and western ducks, and so is the magnificent Black Duck the "gold standard" of the eastern wildfowler. Its wariness and intelligence have enabled it to survive and almost hold its own in the most densely populated areas of the continent. It undoubtedly was one of the first game species to be shot by the original settlers, as it frequents the shores of the eastern seaboard where they landed and hewed out their homes from the forest. And, to this day, it is to be found in the backwoods ponds and streams in the remaining sparsely settled portions of its range.

In the great wilderness of the Labrador peninsula it breeds as completely oblivious of the presence of man as it would on the moon, because over most of that great area there are no men present during the breeding season. Thus it lives in the two extremes of relationship with man. It winters on the thickly populated Atlantic seaboard and west to the Mississippi, and it summers in one of the least known and least travelled regions on the continent, the great triangle of land that stretches eleven hundred miles north from Montreal to Cape Wolstenholme and a thousand miles west from Battle Harbour on the Labrador coast to Moosonee on James Bay, and up the west coast of Hudson's Bay at least as far as the Thelon River. East of the Bay is the principal breeding area, a region of over six hundred thousand square miles, and in it the ducks breed without serious interference from man. The natives are trappers who spend their summers at trading posts on the coast, or about the few posts still operating in the interior. They return to their hunting grounds in the fall just before the freeze-up, and by then the young ducks are awing, and the southward migration has begun.

This vast untouched area is the Black Duck's main stronghold, but it also breeds in numbers farther south in the settled areas of Canada and the northern states. Formerly many birds were produced in the middle Atlantic States, but today the great majority are produced in the north. It is from the southern part of the breeding range that what we know of the breeding habits of the bird has been gleaned. Many a trout fisherman has looked up suddenly at the unexpected whistle of wings of a pair of flaring blacks that have zoomed over him in their strenuous courtship flight, climbing in the blue May sky, silver-lined wings flashing in the brilliant sunshine. That is a sight to stir the blood of the most calloused.

The quiet glide of the canoe along the lilypads of some spruce-rimmed lake in June, when the mosquitoes are getting bad and you are concentrating on keeping your fly moving properly, is often shattered by the loud splash and scurry of a female black frantically feigning injury in front of the bow as her ducklings scatter and race for the weeds. You laugh and toss your fly at her and paddle on around the point and leave her with that precious family in their little cove. As the sun goes down and you are paddling back to camp, trailing a small spinner for bass, you see the ducklings chasing insects among the bulrushes while the mother keeps well outside and, with neck outstretched, keeps her keen eye on the canoe.

Later in the summer as you stand on the Island of Orleans Bridge below Quebec on a still August afternoon, you see rafts of these splendid ducks, with their young now awing, waiting in the main river for dusk before flying into the marsh to feed. They come out of every creek and stream as soon as the young can swim the distance, and out of the back lakes as soon as they can fly, to the great marshes of the St. Lawrence to grow strong for their first long journey south. The Blue-winged Teal already are concentrating in the river marshes and soon will be off, but the hardy blacks are not in such a hurry. They will stay until cold weather forces them to move up stream to the more sheltered waters of Lake St. Peter and the upper river. There they will stay until freeze-up.

It was against such a backdrop that I first came to know and admire Black Ducks more than twenty years ago. That was in 1928, and since then, with the exception of four years of war, I have spent every summer and fall in some of the best breeding areas in southeastern Canada. For the past ten of these twenty years I have kept fairly detailed fieldnotes, and in 1945 when Ducks Unlimited decided to explore the possibilities of extending their operations to the breeding grounds of the Atlantic Flyway, I was engaged as their representative in the Maritimes and Quebec. I was directed to undertake a study of the breeding ecology of the Black Duck to find out what, if anything, could be done to improve breeding conditions in this section of the flyway.

I was on demobilization leave from the Royal Canadian Navy at the time, and I had just returned from the Far East. The routine of getting demobilized from the Navy, acquiring an outfit in wartime, and hiring a man to go with me, delayed the start until mid-July, but on July 16, 1945, the first day's fieldwork was done in the estuary of the St. John River in New Brunswick. The long slow process of gathering data had begun.

Two years later I was able to report to my employers that in my opinion there was no need for habitat improvement projects on the breeding grounds at their present state of stocking. However, there appeared to be a great discrepancy between our knowledge of the breeding ecology of the eastern breeding species and that of those of the western prairies. Until more detailed information was available regarding many points of the Black Duck's breeding ecology, intelligently planned management could not go forward. I therefore recommended that a waterfowl research station similar to the Delta Waterfowl Research Station in Manitoba be set up in eastern Canada to make detailed studies of the breeding waterfowl of the region.

This recommendation was acted upon, and in 1947 the Wildlife Management Institute of Washington, D. C., in cooperation with Ducks Unlimited, the U. S. Fish and Wildlife

Service, and the University of New Brunswick, founded the Northeastern Wildlife Station on the campus of that University at Fredericton. A five-year waterfowl research program was set up and this book contains the results of these studies. It is offered as a basis for future management planning in the eastern section of the Atlantic Flyway in particular, but it also includes data from all parts of the range of the Black Duck.

Chapter I

North and Away!

ONE DAY in early March, the Boston train was pulling into New York City, and it had just crossed the great arched bridge bringing it into the city proper from the suburbs. I was leaning back in my seat and watching the massed ranks of brick and concrete buildings, and giving thanks to God that my lot had not been cast amid these human ant-hills. I was on my way to a meeting of wildlife specialists in Washington, and as the train rolled toward Grand Central Station, and just before it entered the tunnels, my glance fell upon a small point of land jutting out into the harbor. On its extreme end was the only patch of ground in sight which had not been subjugated to mankind with concrete or asphalt, and the reason was soon apparent. On the landward end of the point were the settling ponds of what appeared to be a sewerage disposal plant. Beyond the fenced-in ponds of swirling water were about a hundred yards of field ending in two rocky points of old broken-down stone piers, which extended out into the harbor forming between them a rounded bay of possibly fifty yards in diameter.

In this bay I saw about half a dozen black spots. As I watched with wonder they rose into the air simultaneously with that characteristic upward bound I knew so well, and to confirm their identification, the white flashes of the underwing coverts were visible as they circled to gain altitude, silhouetted against the television aerials of the apartment houses across the water, and headed down the harbor toward the open sea.

Here were wild Black Ducks, one of the most wary and intelligent of all our native game birds, using a small pond near the very heart of one of the greatest metropolitan areas in the world. This was no park where the ducks had become tame by artificial feeding. They were feeding on their normal winter diet of algae and snails on the rocks of the old wharves.

For the rest of my journey I thought long and respectfully about these birds which could live and forage from the barren shores of Labrador and Ungava to the back doors of Manhattan, and I wondered just how much the activities of man really do affect their annual changes in abundance. I decided to follow them through their annual life cycle, and this is what I learned.

Spring Flight

The blacks that flushed from the pond beyond the sewerage disposal plant flew out to the sea and joined the northward movement of all the waterfowl along the coast. This movement starts in February, and the vanguard of the migration keeps pace with the northward movement of the spring thaw. Black Ducks winter from the south coast of Newfoundland and the Atlantic coast of Nova Scotia south to northern Florida and the Mississippi delta, but the birds from the northeastern portions of the breeding grounds winter on the Atlantic seaboard from Newfoundland to Cape Hatteras. Some stragglers stay as far north as open water will permit, as evidenced by a fat and apparently healthy Black Duck shot by an Indian ten miles north of Mingan on the north shore of the Gulf of St. Lawrence on February 20, 1940.

By March 25, in an average year, the migration has reached beyond the coast of southern New Brunswick. Saint John Harbour, Mace's Bay and Musquash Harbour have been full of birds for several weeks, since there has been no open water inland. When there has been open water in the St. John River at Oak Point, it has held a wintering population of American Goldeneyes all winter, and now blacks and Canada Geese have joined them and are crowding the edge of the ice toward Mistake Point. The geese come out to graze in the stubble on the extreme end of Mistake Point, and the advance scouts of the blacks have penetrated 90 miles inland to the head of the estuary at Fredericton by April 1 in their search for open water.

The inland migration from the Mississippi valley and southeastern states has reached southern Ontario about the same time that the coastal migration has reached the head of the Bay of Fundy. By April 15 the whole length of the St. Lawrence has been covered, and the vanguard has reached Anticosti in the Gulf, and Mingan on the North Shore.

Ten days later, or by April 25, they have reached the Strait of Belle Isle, and turn north up the Labrador coast. Sandwich Bay and the Hamilton River valley are reached by May 2, and by the 26th of May they are at Makkovik on the bleak coast north of Hamilton Inlet. Somewhere north of Makkovik and south of the ice-bound Torngat Mountains that parallel the coast to its northern tip at Cape Chidley, the flight must turn across country to reach Ungava Bay since they arrive there in early June. It is not known whether these Ungava Bay birds come from the Atlantic coast or Hudson Bay, but for geographical reasons it seems much more probable that they come across country from the Atlantic seaboard.

I suspect that this turn inland is made somewhere in the vicinity of Nain, as north of Nain the first of the mountains on the coast, the Kiglapait Range, is reached. From there north the coast is most unsuitable for waterfowl habitat as the mountains come down to the open sea with few usable islands off-

shore. The Torngats themselves extend from Saglek Bay almost to Cape Chidley. They are jagged peaks rising directly
from the sea, with deep water close inshore and no suitable
shallows for waterfowl feeding areas. Deep fjords run far inland among the peaks, but they usually terminate in bare rock.

Evergreens disappear along the coast at Cape Mugford, but
dwarf birch and willows grow as far north as the shores of the
fjords among the Torngats, where they rarely reach more than
a few inches above the ground. Even these die out in the region
of McLelan Strait, and from there to Cape Chidley there is
very little vegetation of any sort; the land is predominantly
smooth bare rock (32).

The northernmost extremity of their range has been reached
by June 8, since on this date in 1934 an Eskimo shot three
Black Ducks sixteen miles north of Cape Dorset, Baffin Island.
This is the only known record of the species from north of
Hudson Strait, and this arrival date shows clearly that the
species stays close to salt water on the long spring migration,
as the northernmost stragglers have arrived in Baffin Island
shortly after the break-up of inland waters on the mainland
far to the south.

The break-up at Chimo and George River on the south and
east shores of Ungava Bay occurs usually about June 15, and
not until July 1 at Payne Bay on the west shore of the Bay.
At Kogaluk River in northwestern Ungava the ice may linger
until July 10 in unfavorable years. As we move southward
through the breeding grounds the date of break-up becomes
earlier, and we find that Fort McKenzie on the Kaniapiskau
is open by June 1, and Nitchequon and Mistassini invariably
by May 24. Thus the summer range has received its annual
quota of breeding stock by June 15, and in the more southern
latitudes the great majority of the pairs has left the coast for
the interior lakes before this.

In southern Canada, Black Ducks arrive with the first
puddles of open water; they appear flying over the brown
fields, pockmarked with white patches of unmelted snow and
intertwined with the white ribbons of still frozen creeks and

rivers. As they arrive on the bays and "tickles" of the Labrador coast, they work inland to the mouths of the rivers and streams that flow into the innumerable indentations of the many thousands of miles of coastline. Here they are among the first harbingers of spring that tell the Labradorman it is time to put up the *komatik* sledge and caulk the dory. When break-up comes they disperse in pairs into the vast maze of lakes and streams, forests and rivers, that is the hinterland of the Labrador Peninsula, not to be seen again on the coast until August when they return with their young awing to congregate on salt water before starting south.

The Composition of the Spring Flight

How is this northward moving population made up? Are they single pairs or large unpaired flocks, or both? Several methods of studying the composition of the spring flight were tried at the study area in the estuary of the Saint John River in New Brunswick. The most successful system was to tabulate the ducks seen as paired, unpaired, or as single males. When this tally is plotted as a graph by ten-day periods, the composition of the flight is shown from the date of first arrival to the date of the first hatch. This compilation is shown in Fig. 1 for Black Ducks in the 1949 spring flight on the study area.

This figure shows that the great majority of the early arrivals was paired birds and that the wave of unpaired birds went through between April 10 and 20. After this wave had passed, the percentage paired rose again to 92 per cent of the blacks on the area, and remained above 80 per cent until the spring flight had passed.

Contrast this behavior with that of the American Goldeneye, shown in Fig. 2. The early arrivals also were paired to a very large extent, and the wave of unpaired birds went through between April 10 and 20, as in the blacks; but instead of the percentage paired rising again, as it had risen in the blacks, it dropped steadily until it was down to only 8 per cent by the time the first brood of goldeneyes was hatched. This

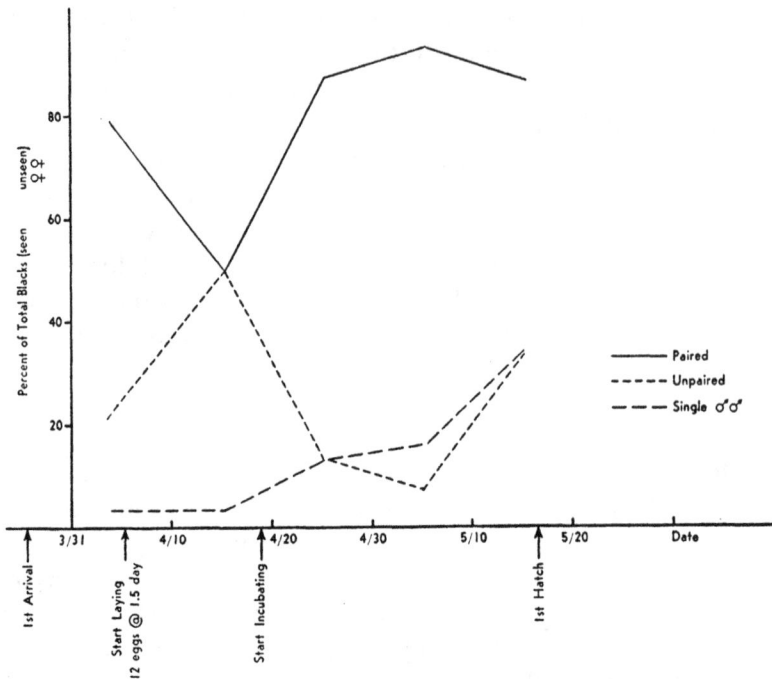

FIG. 1. SPRING FLIGHT—1949—BLACK DUCK
N. B. Study Area—Total Ducks—993

indicates that the vanguard of the goldeneye flight consists of the great majority of the paired birds which pass through the study area going north. The unpaired birds follow and still are passing through in numbers two months after the paired vanguard has passed. This straggling migration of unpaired goldeneyes probably is due to the fact that they do not reach sexual maturity until at least the second breeding season, and the blacks mature the first year. The unpaired blacks pass in a wave, and by the 5th of May they are only 8 per cent of the total. This curve begins to rise again for both species as the pairs break up when incubation becomes well advanced.

In computing these curves the total number of paired birds was found by multiplying the number of pairs by two and adding twice the number of single males observed on territories. Thus the unseen female of the territorial male

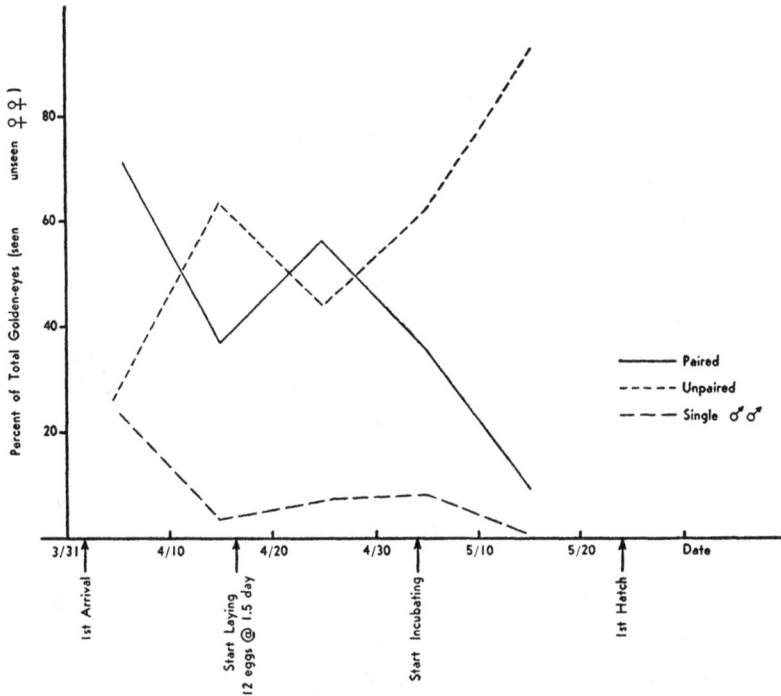

FIG. 2. SPRING FLIGHT—1949—AM. GOLDENEYE
N. B. Study Area—Total Ducks—975

was included. The total of all ducks was computed by adding to the observed total of both sexes the number of unseen females as represented by the number of territorial males.

The local breeders among the first wave of paired blacks settled in and began nesting without delay as laying had started within nine days of the first arrival on the study area. The first blacks arrived on March 28, but the first goldeneyes did not arrive until April 1, and 15 days were spent in courtship and nest hunting before laying was started.

Canada Geese and Wood Ducks arrived on April 6, and Mallards were noted the next day. By the 9th, Green-winged Teal and Ring-necked Ducks had arrived, and by the 15th Blue-winged Teal and Scaup were on hand to complete the spring roster. A few pairs of Pintail drift through later, but none stop and nest, so that in an average year all the nesting species are present by April 15th.

CONDITIONS UPON ARRIVAL ON THE BREEDING GROUNDS

What are conditions like on the northern breeding grounds at this time of year? A graphic picture of conditions in the lower St. Lawrence River when the blacks arrive is given in the Annual Report of the Provancher Society of Quebec (1939, pp. 11). The warden patrolling Basque Island, the Society's sanctuary near Trois Pistoles, has the following entry in his diary for April 16 of that year: ". . . four feet of snow covered the islands in the middle of April . . . Notwithstanding very cold weather and strong north winds 25 Black Ducks, 30 American Eiders, 50 Common Brant, and one Heron were seen on Basque Island . . . although the St. Lawrence was still full of ice." Again on April 10, 1943, "Saw two Black Ducks . . . Still two and a half feet of snow." And on April 5, 1940, "In spite of the snow and ice the Black Ducks have already arrived at the sandbank of Basque Island."

The migrational urge is so strong in them at this season that they drive into sub-Arctic conditions from the St. Lawrence to Ungava Bay, and from the Great Lakes to Baffin Island.

Of the interior of the Labrador peninsula, Low (70) says: "The summer season begins almost simultaneously throughout the interior, and the jump from winter into summer occurs as a rule during the first two weeks of June, when the snow disappears, and the ice leaves the rivers and lakes, except the largest, where it remains until July." He also notes that blacks are not common throughout the interior. From this we may assume that the migration inland from the coast is to the areas adjacent to the shore with decreasing numbers penetrating far inland.

I was told by trappers at North West River, Labrador, however, that they find large rafts of blacks and geese on the big inland lakes when they are on their way to their trap lines in the fall just before freeze-up. These apparently are concentrations of birds which have been in the interior all summer and are about to move out to the coast, or birds migrating overland from Ungava Bay, as there is a goose flight from the north which passes over the Otish Mountains and down the Outardes River. These concentrations are reported as much as two hundred miles from the coast.

That they do not wait for the break-up before moving inland is indicated by Low's record "seen May 1, eggs May 23." He does not give the locale of these reports, but he is discussing the interior, not the coast, at the time.

It will be seen that they are in the very vanguard of the spring migration and that they start north when their breeding grounds still are locked solidly in the grip of winter. The majority spend some time on the coast before they can proceed inland to the breeding lakes, and during this time they court and feed on the sandspits and mudbars uncovered by the movements of the "batteur," or shore ice.

The question of the number of ducks using the interior has been discussed by Hanson et al. for the areas between Lake Mistassini and James Bay (48). These observers travelled by canoe on main canoe routes and saw relatively few ducks. Low also travelled main rivers by canoe and saw very few ducks. However, aerial travel over this country gives a new perspective for the assessment of waterfowl habitat. In June, 1947, I flew from Seven Islands on the Gulf of St. Lawrence to Goose Bay on Lake Melville in the co-pilot seat of a Dakota observing waterfowl habitat, and in August and September, 1948, Dr. Ira N. Gabrielson and I flew from Goose Bay to Fort Chimo on the Koksoak River just south of Ungava Bay. It was obvious from these flights that most of the waterfowl habitat of the country would not be visible to canoeists on the main rivers since it is in the muskeg ponds and lakes that are behind the fringes of scrub spruce lining the banks of the main watercourses. As Low particularly was pressed for time to complete his long journey before freeze-up, he made very few side trips into the surrounding country and confined his work to the main river valleys. It is, therefore, very probable that his estimates, and those of the other canoeists, are conservative.

Eaton (26) says of the valleys of the Slave, Peace, and Little Buffalo Rivers, "From a glance at Table I it is evident that not many ducks or geese appear on the large rivers of the region during at least part of the nesting season (June and July)." He was travelling by canoe and saw 119 ducks on 100 miles of the Slave River between July 1-8, 1940. The Slave River Parklands, an area of 5,000 square miles, was surveyed by air in 1948 by Smith and Allen (135). They estimated an average population density of 4.3 ducks per square mile, and a total population of 21,500. Even allowing for the difference in years, the difference in results is striking. It is, therefore, quite probable that when proper aerial surveys of some of the large areas of swampy lakes and streams in the interior of Labrador and eastern Quebec are made, they will show an appreciable waterfowl production. The breeding population is scattered widely, but the total area is so vast that the annual production probably is the major part of the Atlantic coast flight of blacks, greenwings and goldeneyes, and our banding records show that the region contributes Pintails to the eastern half of the continent, and a few to Europe.

RATES OF TRAVEL

How fast do the migrants travel? An estimate can be made of their rate of progress by taking the straight-line distance between salient points on both the coastal and Hudson Bay migration routes and working out the mileage per day as the dates of departure and arrival at each end are roughly known.

If we assume that on the coastal route the flight leaves from the latitude of the Grand Manan Islands, New Brunswick, on March 25, and we know blacks arrive at the mouth of the George River, Ungava Bay, about June 5, they probably followed the coast around the North Shore of the Gulf of St. Lawrence and northward through the Strait of Belle Isle. The straight-line distances from Grand Manan to Mingan, and from Mingan through the Strait of Belle Isle and north along the coast to Nain, and thence overland to the mouth of the George River on Ungava Bay is about 1,380 miles. This distance has been completed in 72 days, or an average of 19.2 miles per day.

If the flight leaves the latitude of Kingston, Ontario, on the inland route on March 25, and arrives at Cape Dorset, Baffin Island, by June 8, having rounded Cape Jones, Quebec, en route they have covered at least 1,400 miles in 75 days. This is an average of 18.7 miles per day. As none of these flights will be made in a straight line to the end destination as the distances are measured, it is safe to say that they must average at least 20 miles per day for over 70 days to cover the distances involved. However, it is only a small portion of the total breeding population that continues to the northern extremity of the range, and most of the flight drop out at more southerly breeding grounds.

Pairing and Courtship

When do they pair, and what is the manner of their courtship? The question of when Black Ducks pair has been discussed by Sawyer (109), Townsend (128), and by Trautman (130). Trautman witnessed pairing and courtship, including copulation in adults, as early as September at Put-in-Bay, Ohio. He also observed young of the year indulging in courtship display in their first fall.

On August 7, 1946, I observed about one hundred blacks at the Island of Orleans bridge on the St. Lawrence below Quebec. When first seen these birds were sleeping on the rocks at low tide. They were large birds mostly with reddish feet and legs and yellowish bills, but some were much smaller with olive-green bills and brownish feet, and I assumed that they were young of the year. I could see as they stood on the boulders with heads under their wings that the adults definitely were in two's. I stalked to within 70 yards to observe foot and bill color with binoculars, but when I attempted to get closer over bare mud they saw me and flushed. They also were paired when flying.

On August 19 and 20, 1946, at Tabusintac Lagoon on the north coast of New Brunswick, I observed blacks flying in pairs, and one pair seen at close range while resting appeared to be adults. This would seem to indicate that the adults pair directly after the female has completed her moult.

On Prince Edward Island on August 23, 1946, I collected a pair of immature birds which were observed carrying on the head-bob phase of the courtship display. Close to the courting pair collected were two males displaying before a female, and all three appeared to be young of the year. The gonads of the immature male collected were 8 mm. in length, or normal for that time of year. Its immature tail feathers had been almost all replaced, however, even at that early date.

At Ox Island in the St. John River in New Brunswick on August 29, 1946, I collected one of a pair of blacks that were sleeping side by side on the end of a mud bar. One bird was standing with its head under its wing and the other was lying beside it. I selected the standing bird as the best target as I was shooting a scope-sighted .22 rifle. A sixty-yard crawl was necessary to get within certain range, and at the shot the standing bird flopped to the water and the other jumped into the air. The flying bird circled and came back to the cripple twice, and left for good only upon seeing me running up to dispatch the wounded bird. It was an immature male with gonads 5.5 mm. long. The other bird was the smaller of the two, and I concluded it was a female from the typical female quacks it uttered as it flew around the wounded male.

This evidence, in support of Trautman's, suggests that the young of the year pair, at least temporarily, at the end of their first summer. That this pairing is either not permanent, or only indulged in by a portion of the young birds, is suggested by the unpaired flocks that arrive during the spring flight, and it also is possible that this supposed pairing of young is the remnant of a brood in the process of breaking up. The courtship display, however, gives it definite sexual significance whether the partners were brood mates or not.

On October 31, 1953, my guide and I were sitting beside

a small beaver pond on the headwaters of the Nipisiguit River trying to get a bull moose to answer the call. A pair of Black Ducks fed in the pond in front of us for more than half an hour at not more than 30 yards where the difference in bill color of the male and female was plain to see with the naked eye. This was confirmed with 10 x binoculars, and the male uttered the typical reedy quack many times. These birds were feeding, and no courtship activity was observed. They were a solitary pair on a small pond in the deep forest at a time when the southward migration was in full swing.

It appears, therefore, that the only time of year when the adult female is not paired or being courted is when she actually is hatching out her eggs at the end of the incubation period, rearing her brood, and moulting. As soon as her moult is completed she joins the males and is paired off again shortly thereafter. The young females are courted and pair at least temporarily at the end of their first summer. The young males have developed sexual interest in the females, at least to the point of courtship display, although copulation has not been observed, by the end of their first summer.

As a large percentage of the total population of blacks arriving in the spring are paired (see Fig. 1), the greater part of the young birds must pair on the winter range during their first winter. This is further supported by the observations of the beginning of sexual interest among the young in their first fall.

The courtship of the Black Duck has been described in considerable detail by Sawyer (*ibid.*), Townsend (*ibid.*), and Trautman (*ibid.*). Townsend's description is as follows, and it agrees closely with the observations on the study area in New Brunswick: "A group of fifteen or twenty may be seen solemnly feeding by dipping, with their tails pointing zenithwards, when they begin to swim about nervously, weaving their way in and out among their fellows. Now one swims rapidly with head low and darts at another that, in order to avoid him, dives just below the surface with a great splashing of his wings. Soon nearly the whole group are chasing each other and diving awkwardly. Every now and then the short quack of the drake is heard, sometimes the loud croak of the duck. Now a drake flies fifteen or twenty feet over the water with drooping body and legs and plumps down by a duck with an impetus that carries him three or four feet farther. This is repeated again and again by the drakes and is a con- spicious part of the courtship. At times they bob the head in a manner exactly similar to that already described in the case of the Mallards. The bobbing does not continue so long, for the short flight seems to play a more important part in the courtship of the Black Duck. It is possible that the white lower surface of the wing revealed in these short flights may have an entrancing effect upon the females. It is a common courtship action, however, even with birds whose under-wing surface is not conspicuous and, it seems to me, these flights are very different from the pursuit in the air of the female by one or more males. The short flights are courtship display for the purpose of attracting the female and leading to a choice. The pursuit flights are different and are not in the nature of a display; it is possible indeed that the choice had already been made."

Bent (14) describes the courtship, or pursuit flight, as fol- lows: "Near some woodland reservoir I have heard the loud quacking notes and looking up, I have seen a pair or perhaps three, of these ducks flying over the tree tops at full speed; the courtship flight seems to be a test of speed and energy, a sort of aerial game of tag, as they sweep around again and again in a large circle or back and forth over the pond or swamp which they will probably choose for their summer home; finally the bride yields to the suitor of her choice and they fly off together or drop down into the water."

This behavior is similar to that observed many times on the study area in New Brunswick, but the pursuit flight often has been confused with that of a drake defending his territory against an intruding pair, rather than two drakes pursuing a female. The pursuing drakes have been observed to catch the female by the tail feathers in the air; she then side-slipped

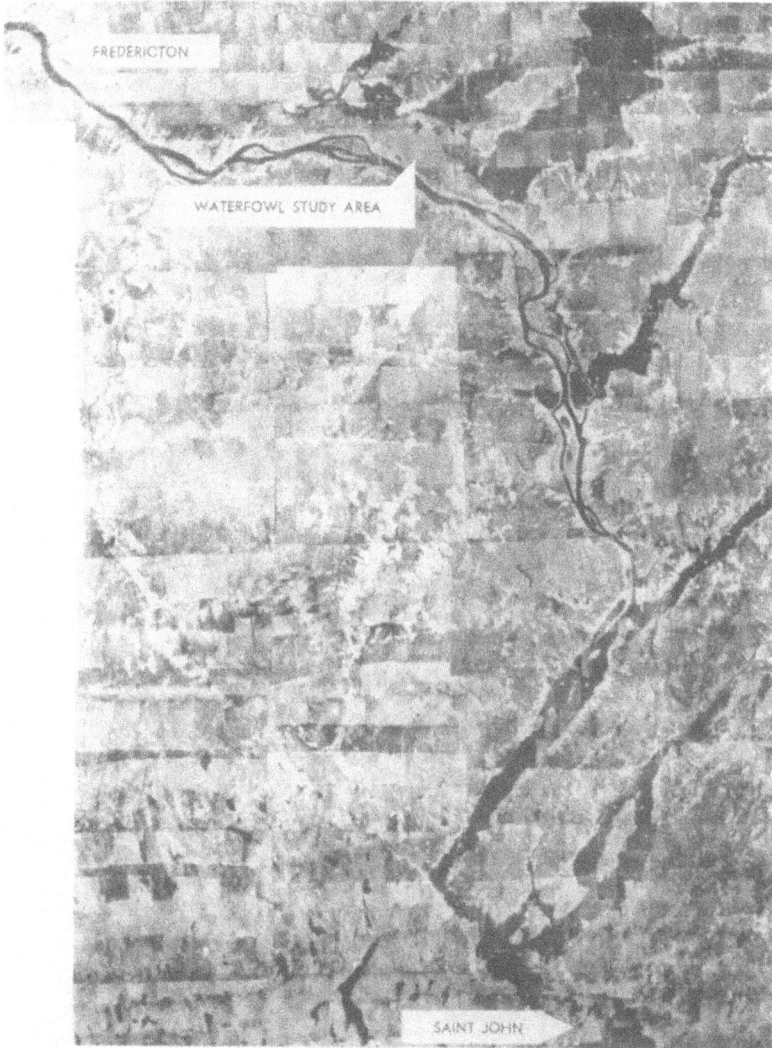

Plate I. The estuary of the St. John River in New Brunswick, one of the great funnels into the interior. Fredericton to Saint John by river is about 90 miles, and the head of tidewater is a few miles above Fredericton. The main spring flight leaves the estuary below the limit of tidewater and travels across country about 80 miles to the Gulf of St. Lawrence and the breeding ducks of central New Brunswick drop out as the flight goes through.

Plate II. The bleak outer coast of Newfoundland and Labrador offers little food or shelter for waterfowl on the long flight north.

Photo by W. H. Carrick

Plate III. They migrate in spring in small parties, and usually at a considerable height.

Photo by W. H. Carrick

Plate IV. Black Ducks courting. The head of the male is considerably more massive than that of the female at this of year.

violently and apparently jerked her tail free, with the drakes, as many as four at a time, in hot pursuit. This tail pulling is described and illustrated by Hochbaum (55) for Canvasbacks, Redheads and Lesser Scaup. It has not been observed in any other species but Black Ducks in New Brunswick.

THE MATING PERIOD

When does the actual mating take place? The period of copulation has been shown by Trautman (*ibid.*) to begin in September. In the fall, copulation seems to occur more frequently on warm days, and during the winter no attempts at copulation were observed. It is resumed again as the days begin to lengthen at the approach of spring, and on March 29, I made the following observation at a pool of open water in one of the small channels of the still solidly frozen St. John River in New Brunswick.

At 3 p.m. on this day the female of a pair of blacks stopped feeding and swam into an open space between the edge of the ice and the bank and assumed the "neck stretch" position (55). The male joined her immediately, and they both performed the head bob display for about one minute. The male then mounted briefly four times, but each time either fell off or jumped off almost at once and dived. He rose in the water and flapped his wings and bathed by ducking each time after he attempted to mount. He then swam half around the female at high speed in the "sneak" position (55) and mounted for the fifth time. This time the female submerged almost completely, and the male remained covering her for about five seconds, holding her with his bill by the back of the neck and chewing hard. When they separated they both bathed by ducking and flapping their wings, and then swam over to shallow water and stood on a mud bank and preened. All sexual excitement seemed over, and five minutes later the female began feeding again. The male did not begin feeding for 15 minutes but remained on the alert with head held high.

The following day, copulation was observed in another pair without any preliminaries whatsoever, and it seemed to be successful at the first attempt. Fast swimming in the "sneak" position around the female was performed after copulation in this case, followed by washing and wing flapping.

The whole procedure from the first act of sexual excitement, the "neck stretch" of the female, to the disengaging of the pair did not take more than five minutes, and the second observation was considerably shorter. It is for this reason that actual observations of copulation are difficult to make in the wild.

Defense of the Female

What is the relation of the pairs to others of their kind? Friction among males was noted upon several occasions, but pairs of blacks fed within 20 feet of each other, and often less, without any noticeable display of jealousy. They were noted to approach pairs of Wood Ducks and Green-winged Teal with none paying any attention to the others.

Hybrids of Mallard and Black Duck have been found on many occasions in the northeast so that this cross must occur, but presumably the pair was formed on the southern wintering grounds, where Mallards are more plentiful, as they are very scarce on the breeding grounds in the northeast.

An instance of a male defending its mate to the point of pursuing its rival in the air is given in my field notes as follows: "4/25/49, Oromocto Flats, N. B.

A pair in a roadside pond was approached by a single male. The paired male first herded the female away from the intruder, and then both males jumped from the pond and flew at high speed in a circle, the paired male chasing the other. The intruder finally landed in another pond on the far side of the road, whereupon the paired male returned to its mate."

Paired males will tolerate other pairs, but the approach of an unpaired male is the signal for violent reaction. The female does not appear to take any interest in the proceedings, but continues feeding or resting quietly. Pairs of other species are tolerated near the female, but unpaired Pintail drakes have been observed to be driven off.

COVER REQUIREMENTS DURING SPRING FLIGHT

Where would you look for blacks at various hours of the day in spring? Observations were made of the different habitats used by the ducks at various times of the day during spring flight. At daylight the majority of blacks was to be found feeding in the flooded potholes and creeks of the fields along the river valley. As the sun became fully visible they left the fields and flew to the flooded timber of the river islands and timbered swamps. They stayed in this excellent cover, sleeping and resting throughout the day, and seldom were seen in open water until dusk.

The goldeneyes, on the other hand, are almost always in open water, and for the first three hours of daylight they are found in single pairs or courting groups. Later they gather in flocks in the deep water of rivers and lakes where they stay together until dusk when the flocks again break up into pairs.

Wood Ducks are not often seen in the wet fields, but stay near the edge of the flooded timber where they may be found at any hour of the day. The two teals remain in the flooded fields most of the day, but the Ring-necked Ducks stay in the open water with the goldeneyes.

This pattern is followed in the cultivated areas of southern Canada only. When the flight enters the northern forest, the habitat is the stream and lake type of the Precambrian Region of the Canadian Shield, and areas of muskeg and floating bogs are preferred locations in many areas.

SPRING FOODS

Let us now turn to what is perhaps the most important single factor in the whole complex picture of the long flight north. What foods are available at this time of year between the Maine coast and Ungava Bay?

The work of Mendall in Maine has shown in great detail what foods are eaten by blacks in that state at all seasons of the year (80). He has shown that while on the winter range along the coast they feed on 86.9 per cent animal food consisting of snails, periwinkles, limpets, miscellaneous clams and mussels, amphipods, and even small fish. The remaining 13.1 per cent of vegetable food was composed of marine algae, sea lavender, cord grass, pigweed, sea blite and other, unidentified, plant material. This diet probably remains essentially the same, with local additions and subtractions, up the Atlantic seaboard to the northern limit of the range. It is when the blacks move inland to fresh water that the major change in their diet takes place.

The spring runoff is just beginning as they arrive on the study area in southern New Brunswick, and the snow is disappearing from the cultivated lands. As the river ice breaks up and the rising flood reaches the fields, an increasing row of seeds gathers along the edge of the rising water. When the water has covered mile-wide fields this row of seeds may be three or four feet wide around the edge of the flood. It is on this row that the blacks and other dabbling ducks feed when they arrive. Their diet changes overnight from the 85 per cent animal matter on the coast, to over 90 per cent vegetable matter when they reach the interior. In Maine, Mendall's figures were 92.6 per cent vegetable foods and 7.4 per cent animal foods. Seeds of sedges, various rushes, bullrushes, and burreed made up the greater part of the vegetable food. Various insects, snails and mollusks made up the animal food.

In the St. John valley where all the bottomlands are cultivated, the principal seeds are the residue of the previous year's crop, and Plates VI and VII show a favorite feeding area during spring migration which was a field of timothy during the summer months.

An interesting spring feeding habit of both blacks and Canada Geese in Laborador was described to the writer at North West River. Local hunters alleged that the early spring arrivals of ducks and geese often were found to be feeding on the southern exposures of the hills far from water as soon as the snow melted sufficiently to show some bare ground. They were feeding on blueberries which had remained on the bushes all winter under the snow and were exposed by the spring thaw. It was stated that the ducks and geese were so full of these berries that the hands were stained while cleaning them. I did not see this behavior as I was not there at that season, but it was told as a well-known local phenomenon which was used to advantage by the hunters.

How much does a Black Duck eat at one meal? Present methods of stomach analysis do not give accurate answers to this question as all that is found in the digestive tract is the unassimilated and half-digested material that was going through when the bird was shot. Thus the total volume found in the bird always is less than the volume actually eaten. How much less depends upon the elapsed time since eating stopped. The amount of material found in 59 stomachs collected from New Brunswick to Ungava Bay, between April and October, averaged 7.22 cc. per stomach. The maximum found was 20.00 cc., and the minimum of identifiable material was considered to be 1.00 cc. Many stomachs were empty, and they were not included in this compilation.

The time of day the specimen is collected also has an important bearing on the results of stomach analysis in the Black Duck. Most of the feeding is done at night, in the very early morning, or late evening. Thus, to obtain the maximum number of full stomachs per birds collected, the collecting should be confined to the early morning hours. This was not done in the present study as the observers were in the field all day and collected specimens as opportunity afforded for other purposes than stomach analysis. No specimens were taken specifically for a food habits study, but stomachs were examined as routine from all specimens taken for any purpose, as well as those taken from muskrat traps in the spring.

An interesting observation on the spring food habits of the species on the north coast of New Brunswick was related by Mr. J. Wishart of Tabusintac, New Brunswick, a well-known guide and outfitter of that region. He reports that the major food of the blacks in that area during early spring is herring eggs. The spawning run of the herring is underway when the bulk of the Black Duck migration is passing through, and he reports collecting specimens whose crops and gizzards contained nothing else. This habit also was reported in Labrador, and presumably is common all up the coast.

The strong predilection for animal food in the spring diet on the coast is illustrated further by the results of an attempt to introduce frogs on the Island of Anticosti in the Gulf of St. Lawrence. Reptiles and amphibians are not native to the island, and the owner attempted to introduce frogs in the hope that they would help control the insect pests which were in their normal abundance in the northern forests. The attempt was a failure because flocks of Black Ducks devoured the tadpoles and young frogs as fast as they hatched in the spring (58). The waterfowl habitat on Anticosti is mainly along the south coast, but as the width of the island is only about 34 miles, the whole of the inland swamps and ponds are within reach of the coastal concentration of birds and it does not seem practicable here to distinguish between coastal and interior diets.

In the region of Lake St. Peter on the St. Lawrence the blacks are to be found feeding in the fields well above flood waters after the manner of stubble Mallards in the west shortly after they arrive in the spring. This is unusual in eastern Canada, and I have not recorded this habit elsewhere. These birds apparently come overland from the lower part of the New England seaboard.

It will be seen, therefore, that availability seems to be the greatest single factor in their choice of spring foods, and that they are truly omnivorous birds changing from a predominantly animal diet on the coast to a predominantly vegetable diet as soon as they reach the interior.

Forbush (33) states that fresh water is a requirement of the species and that if they are using salt marshes they must go once or twice daily to fresh water to drink. However, Gross (44) found two adults and a brood on Mark Island off the Maine coast, and another nest on a second island, neither of which contained fresh water. It is possible that dew and rain supplied sufficient fresh water for these birds, but the observations were inconclusive on this point.

Mortality During Spring Flight

What are the mortality factors they must face? Accidental mortality among blacks in spring flight appears to be rather rare. During World War II torpedoed ships were brought into Halifax streaming oil from their shattered hulls, and many seabirds were killed by entering the oil slick. However, Black Ducks seemed to be only slightly affected as only one carcass of this species was picked up (67).

Predation data secured on the study area are rather scarce. On more than one occasion a Bald Eagle was observed to fly over a raft of migrating blacks, Canada Geese, Blue-winged and Green-winged Teal, and they flushed as the eagle approached. The eagle paid no attention to them and continued on a straight course, although they were making violent efforts to get out of its way. On May 7, 1948, feathers of a Wood Duck were found at the mouth of an occupied fox den, and again on May 11 the wing and body feathers of a female ringneck were found at the mouth of the same den. Apparently this particular vixen made a practice of hunting ducks, and presumably caught them by stalking when the birds were asleep on the logs and debris along the shore. She also brought many frogs to the den. The river bottomlands, particularly the islands which are not covered during the flood, have a high fox population at this writing, so that this form of predation may be fairly heavy during the period of spring flight.

Spring shooting still is carried on as a necessary source of food in northern Newfoundland, Labrador, and by the natives of the Eastern Arctic. On Lake Melville this shooting is done from white canoes among the breaking ice, and the birds are stalked and shot on the water in as large numbers as possible as ammunition is scarce and expensive. The Indians still are in the interior at the time this shoot takes place, and they kill very few ducks for this reason. The coastal population of Labradormen and Eskimos hunt the waterfowl as their only source of fresh meat at that season. The failure of this supply has resulted in outbreaks of beri-beri and other diseases of malnutrition, and on some occasions in actual starvation.

The total kill made in this manner is not large when compared to the kill of sportsmen on some of the better-known duck shooting areas farther south, but as it occurs just before the nesting season, the loss in productivity of the region is considerable. As large-scale mining developments are planned for the interior of Labrador, the human population may be expected to increase. Unless modern methods of supply increases proportionately, this drain on the breeding stock of the flyway may be increased materially, and any waterfowl management plan for the area should pay close attention to this problem. As the matter of human survival is at stake here, rather than purely recreational values, it would be neither prudent nor profitable to attempt to enforce the Migratory Bird Convention Act too strongly in this region, at least until another source of fresh meat becomes available in early spring.

A serious mortality factor which can be controlled by man is spring muskrat trapping. The total kill of ducks in muskrat traps in Maine in 1946 was conservatively estimated to be 1,945, with an additional 2,220 injured but released alive (37). The heaviest mortality among females was in Ring-necked Ducks and Mergansers. Black Ducks, which made up 43 per cent of all ducks taken, were about equally divided as to sex. As a result of this study the Maine legislature authorized a muskrat trapping season in the fall, but so far it has not abolished the spring season. It is hoped that the other governments concerned will follow suit in the near future, but this will not be done until there is a strong public demand for such action.

Fall muskrat trapping is not popular with the trappers in some of the Maritime Provinces now because there are other things the trapper can do at this season. But in the spring he has a slack period which traditionally is spent in muskrat trapping. This long-established custom will be the greatest stumbling block to legal action to change the season to the fall. Maine has set the precedent and taken the first step, but much educational work will be required before New Brunswick will be willing to follow.

The number of ducks killed in this manner is in direct proportion to the intensity of trapping in the region, and will, therefore, be greater in the northern states and southern Canada than in the northern areas where the intensity of trapping is much less. A recent estimate of the population density of the eastern Arctic shows that in the Ungava district and offshore islands there is one Eskimo for every 43 square miles and 2 miles of coastline (105). This undoubtedly is a higher density than that of the Indian hunting grounds farther south in the interior, and the Indians are the principal muskrat trappers of the region. It appears unlikely therefore, that muskrat trapping would be a serious mortality factor north of the St. Lawrence, but in the northern states and Maritime Provinces its abolition would be a decided forward step in waterfowl management.

The dangers the waterfowl must face in the long northward journey begin with occasional predation from Bald Eagles, which also are moving north to their summer range, and foxes, minks, and Great Horned Owls on the lowlands of southern Canada. In this region many are lost to muskrat traps, but this loss begins to decrease as the birds cross the St. Lawrence. As they leave the danger area of muskrat trappers they enter the zone where they are again concentrated along the coast as the interior has not yet broken up. Here they are preyed upon by the spring hunters of Labrador and Ungava until break-up allows them to leave the coast for the solitude and peace of the interior lakes where they may never see a man. Throughout almost their whole range they have one enemy to contend with which will kill ducks at every opportunity; that is the Great Horned Owl. These owls always are solitary or in pairs and do not concentrate as do the eagles in the estuary of the St. John. If they did, their predation on ducks could be very serious indeed, as individual owls have taken a serious toll of a local population of waterfowl.

Chapter II

The Forest Duck

HOW MUCH time is wasted after arrival before getting down to housekeeping? Nest building begins in southern New Brunswick almost as soon as the ducks reach the breeding ground, since laying has started only nine days after the first arrivals have landed. The drake is led by his hen back to her traditional breeding area, where she begins hunting for a nest site. In areas of constant water levels and high population densities the Black Duck appears to be just as exacting a territorial species as its near relative, the Mallard. However, in most areas in the northeast, the breeding population is scattered widely, and the water level fluctuates violently; so it is not only unnecessary, but almost impossible, for the drake to defend one specific area as his territory throughout the entire period of territorial defense.

In this region the drake often defends a section of shore-line as his territory against intrusion by all other males of his own species. However, he rarely has the opportunity to remain on his selected area for the whole period as he may find it two feet under water one day, and half a mile from water three or four days later as the flood ebbs and flows. This situation is shown in Plate IX. He then is forced to move to some adjacent area.

The maximum period a male black was observed to defend one area in New Brunswick was 13 days, and this was observed only once in four breeding seasons. The average period of defense of one particular area is much less, and the drake may have had to change his territory several times. The drake usually was observed on his territory in the afternoon and evening, and was absent in the morning. When on the territory the pair show a fearlessness which is quite unusual in Black Ducks. One year a pair established a territory on the side of the right-of-way of the Trans-Canada Highway where it crosses the Oromocto Flats and occupied it within 10 yards of fairly heavy traffic. The birds would stay on the bank when a car passed within 10 yards as long as the car did not stop, but as soon as the car stopped they swam out into the channel. The distance between the two extreme points on the highway where the pair, or the drake, was observed was 97 yards. Again in forest pools the territory may be as small as 25 feet in diameter, so the size is extremely variable and depends upon the nature of the site selected.

As almost all water areas in the northeast at this time of year have abundant logs, hummocks, and stumps on their shoreline, the requirement for a loafing bar stressed by Hochbaum (55) as a necessary component of a territory in the west, is not a problem. Water seems to be the only requirement beside a freedom from interference by man. The cover requirements also seem to have the widest possible limits as territories were occupied in flood waters in an open field and in a beaver pond surrounded by dense forest to the waterline. No instance of the occupation of a new beaver pond was recorded, but several were occupied while still in use and before any submerged or emergent aquatics had become established. In those instances feeding must be done to a large extent outside the territory. As Benson (13) has pointed out, the black is typically a bird of the beaver pond ecology at this time of year when its coloring blends well with the deep black and brown shadows affording it a maximum of protection.

The period in which territories are selected and established and nest sites are chosen can be determined fairly accurately from the data on hand. This calculation is shown below.

BLACK DUCK PRE-NESTING AND NESTING CHRONOLOGY,
Study Area, N. B. (4-year period)

Average date of arrival . . . . 87th day of the year, March 28.

Average date first brood . . . . 136th day, May 16.

Incubation period . . . . 28 days (14).

:.Date clutch complete . . . . 108th day, April 18.

Clutch average—
    9 at 1.33 days per egg . . . . 12 days laying period (14).

:.Date first egg . . . . 96th day, April 6.

:.Pre-Nesting Period . . . . 9 days.

Laying period (first eggs) . . . . April 6—April 18.

Incubation period (first eggs) . . . . April 18—May 16.

Overall first nesting period . . . . April 6—May 16.

This calculation is based on one sharp observational date, the date of first brood, and the other factors which already are known and whose source is indicated. The date of first brood on the study area in New Brunswick has been remarkably uniform. The average date for the first four years of the study was May 16, and the over-all span of the dates was only four days. The maximum deviation from the average was only two days. There is, therefore, a fairly solid basis from which to work out the pre-hatching chronology for an average year.

From the above it will be seen that the first territories have been established and nest sites selected in the nine days immediately after arrival, which has been the period March 28-April 6 for the four years under study.

THE PERIOD OF FERTILIZATION

When are the eggs fertilized? As the limit of life of the
sperm in the oviduct is thought to be about two weeks,
copulation prior to two weeks before the date of first egg
would have no significance.

Bent quotes Robert T. Moore saying that in a nest containing 12 eggs, three were laid in the last four days. This is a laying rate of 0.75 eggs per day. Thus 1.33 days is the time required for one egg to pass through the oviduct and out through the cloaca. Therefore, on the study area the period in which fertilization must occur for first eggs on April 6 is from March 23 (April 6 −14 days) to one day before laying, or April 5.

The duration of daylight in 45 degrees North latitude on March 27 is 12 hours, 30 minutes, and on April 6 it is 13 hours. Rowan (108), Bissonnette (15 & 16), and others have pointed out that there is increasing evidence that seasonal sexual reproduction in certain plants and animals is more or less conditioned by the relative lengths of day and night, by the intensity of the illumination, and in some cases by the color and wave length of the light to which they are exposed. This would indicate that spermatogenesis in Black Ducks of this region has a light threshold of about 12½ hours of daylight as the large majority of the year's first eggs are fertilized in the period immediately about March 30, although the pair may have been together all winter.

THE SIGNIFICANCE OF SPRING PHENOLOGY ON THE BREEDING CYCLE

What effect has the state of advancement of spring at the nest site upon the date of first eggs? A careful record of spring phenology was made in the five-year period 1945-1949 to determine what effect, if any, the phenological and meteorological conditions of the five seasons had upon the breeding cycle of the Black Duck. The results of this study can be summed up in a few sentences.

The break-up of the St. John River in the period under discussion varied by three weeks. The date of last frost varied by 15 days. The mean temperature for the month of April varied by 9.1 degrees, and that of May by 3.1 degrees. Precipitation in the month of April varied 58 per cent, and in May 170 per cent. Black Ducks arrived on the study area in an over-all period of 13 days; yet despite these large differences in the phenology and meteorology of the area, the over-all period in which the first broods appeared for four years was only four days. This strongly suggests that local weather conditions and the stage of advancement of spring at the nest site have little influence on the breeding cycle, and that the first eggs are fertilized and will be laid at very nearly the same dates each year quite independent of the weather conditions on the breeding grounds when the birds arrive. Exceptionally bitter weather may, however, turn the migrants away from their traditional breeding grounds, and this probably is one cause of the ebb and flow of populations on individual marshes.

As the first eggs are laid only nine days after arrival, and fertilization takes place up to 14 days before laying, it seems very likely that many eggs are fertilized at long distances from the site of laying. This is further reason to doubt that weather on the breeding ground has a serious influence on the date the first eggs are laid.

The Selection of the Nest Site

Where do Black Ducks nest? The nest sites are selected by the female and vary widely with the type of terrain. In the lowlands of the St. John River, and no doubt in other areas in eastern Canada, the nest frequently is placed in holes and crotches in mature hardwoods. These tree nests are numerous along Portobello Creek on the study area, which is the first place they have been recorded as common.

The ground nesting area begins above the peak water level of the flood, which is at the rear of the bottomland cultivation. This area includes the upland pasture of the valley sides and extends as far as two miles into the mixed-wood second growth of the uplands. An accurate observation of the distance these nests are placed back in the woods was made when a female with a newly hatched brood was observed to come out to a woods road and start down it for the main river. The distance to the river from the point where she reached the road was measured on the car speedometer as 2.1 miles.

Photo by B. C. Carter

Plate V. Daytime resting cover during spring migration. The flooded hardwoods of the river islands where the blacks sleep during the middle of the day on the St. John River, New Brunswick.

Plate VI. Spring foods. As the farmer leaves it in the fall . . .

Plate VII. . . . and as the ducks use it during the spring flight.

Plate VIII. Perhaps the greatest single cause of spring mortality among the breeding ducks of southeastern Canada and the adjacent States. A Wood Duck caught in a muskrat trap set on a floating log.

Plate IX. A territory as it was selected, and as it was abandoned four days later.

Plate X. A territory in an occupied beaver pond with dense forest to the waterline.

Plate XI. A completed clutch showing the down wall around the eggs.

Photo by W. H. Carrick

Plate XII. A nest in plain view on top of a stump.

Photo by R. C. Carter

Plate XIII. Tree-nest hunting in the flooded lowlands. Portobello Creek,
New Brunswick.

Plate XIV. A typical tree nest site. The nest is in the hollow core of the dead stub in the center of the fork.

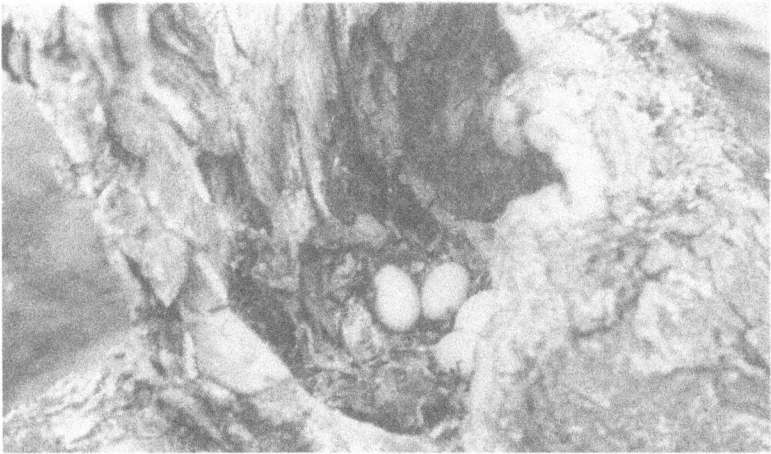

Plate XV. Typical tree nest on Portobello Creek, in overmature Silver Maple. *(Acer saccharinum).*

Plate XVI. A tree nest twenty feet above water.

Photos by R. L. Mosher

Plate XVII. Typical Montagnais Indians at North West River Post, Labrador.

In the woods the nests are located near brush piles and in clumps and thickets. Tussocks in wet places in the upland pastures also are favored locations. Bent quotes Samuels as saying that he once found a nest on a low stump which was one mile from any water, and Frazar that in Labrador the nests are placed upon the outspreading branches of stunted spruces. At this time of year the black might well be called the "forest duck" as it is to be found in the deep woods far from the famous shooting places where the sportsman is accustomed to seeing it.

The lowlands below the level of the peak flood comprise the tree nesting area. Bent quotes Edwin Beaupre as saying that two tree nests were found on the St. Lawrence, one in an old crow's nest, and one in the last year's nest of a Red-shouldered Hawk. The lowland hardwoods which border the main channel of the St. John and cover the river islands are submerged to a depth of 10 feet during the flood, and it is in the holes and crotches in these trees that the nests are built. They usually are in overmature trees, and silver maple (*Acer saccharinum*) is a preferred species on the study area. The height of the nest above water varies as the flood rises and falls. The highest found was about 20 feet above the water the day it was found, but at the time it was built the water level had been higher.

In the Portobello area the nests often are situated in trees which are a mile or more from any dry land during the nesting period. As there is very little food available in the flooded timber when the water is 10 or more feet deep, it seems probable that the female must fly at least a mile to the edge of the flood to feed. It is here that the drake has established a territory and awaits her for the greater part of the incubation period.

A Black Duck was found nesting in a tree which had been used the year before. The second year the nest was in a hole higher up the tree than the site used the first year since the previous site was flooded out. It is interesting to speculate whether or not this was the same bird. It seems probable that

it was as there were many sites available around that particular tree, and there was no apparent reason why it should
be selected two consecutive years by two separate birds. A
ground nest was found on Prince Edward Island under a
small spruce on a golf course. There had been a nest within
50 yards of that spruce every year for more than 10 years,
according to the groundsman of the course, and he believes
that the duck was the same bird each year. As banding records
show that the life span of the species is at least 17 years, this
is possible. The work of Sowls (115) at the Delta Station in
Manitoba, shows the persistence with which certain individuals
will return to their chosen nesting areas. One shoveller hen
renested twice in one year after her first nest was robbed deliberately, and returned to the area to nest the following year.

THE DURATION OF THE NESTING PERIOD

The duration of the nesting period has been traced from
records of more than 101 nests in the literature and on the
study area. These data are presented in Appendix I.

They show a spread in nesting dates from March 15 to
July 3, with the peak nesting in the month of May. The area
covered is from Virginia to Labrador, and it is interesting to
note that the earliest nest record from this large range of
latitude is not to be found in the south, but in the Grand
Manan Islands of New Brunswick. These islands are a well-
known wintering ground for numbers of Black Ducks, and
this nesting female may not have migrated that season.

As shown previously, the average date of the first egg on
the study area in New Brunswick is April 6. Nesting builds
up to a peak in May and tapers off through June with a few
renesting attempts extending into July. This pattern seems
to be followed closely whether the duck nests in Virginia or
Labrador, which is further evidence that the local weather
conditions have only slight influence on the physiological
condition of the female.

THE COMPOSITION OF THE NEST

Of what are the nests made? Nest building and laying take

place almost simultaneously as the female selects the site and lays the first egg when the nest consists only of a slight hollow surrounded by the adjacent cover. The nest consists of the material at hand built into a compact wall around the eggs and lined with down. As the clutch grows the nest increases in size, and the amount of down increases until the last egg is laid. Such material as twigs, dead ferns, white birch leaves, stems of goldenrod, and sedges have all been observed in ground nests. Tree nests usually are made of punk, bark, and down. When the female leaves the nest to forage she covers the eggs with the down, but if she is flushed from the nest she often defecates on the eggs. This may be due to fright, or it may be a deliberate attempt to camouflage the eggs, which she has not had time to cover.

Mousley (84) noted a difference in the manner in which the female left a ground nest as incubation advanced. In the early stages she left the nest with an upward spring, but as incubation advanced she left by sailing away very low for some distance before rising. This appears to be a definite attempt to hide the location of the nest as her annual gamble of bringing off a family is nearing completion.

The tell-tale strands of down hanging from the lip of a hole in some dead stub is the sign the tree-nest hunter looks for as he paddles his canoe through the flooded timber. The nest may be that of a black, a goldeneye, or a Wood Duck, but a glance at the down will tell him which, even though the eggs are too far down the hole to be seen and the female is not about. The down of the Black Duck has a distinct brownish hue, and almost always has a few breast feathers in it which have been plucked out with the down. Broley (19) gives a key for the identification of down which is very useful in this work.

Tree-nest hunting in the flooded timber is an occupation not without some hazard. Climbing irons are necessary to reach many nests, and the tree is rotten or it would not have a hole in it. During the ascent to the nest it is possible that the nest hunter and the tree both may topple into 10 feet of icy water more than a mile from any solid ground. For this reason tree-nest examinations never should be attempted when alone.

When the clutch has hatched successfully the membrane sacks from the eggs will be found complete and looking like rumpled bags with particles of shell sticking to them. If the nest has been robbed by a predator the membrane will be found still securely attached to the interior of the shell, with the caved-in edges of the broken shell sticking to it and not loose in the nest.

The size of the clutch is given by Bent as 6 to 12, and the study area data averaged nine. The eggs themselves are a greenish buff in color without spots, and 82 eggs averaged 59.4 x 43.2 mm. (14). The incubation period is given as 26 to 28 days, which checks well with Mousley's observation in which he had a clutch under observation for 25 days before it hatched. Bent also gives a detailed description of the hatching process, quoting Charles F. Allen (1893), and says that the young leave the nest one to three hours after hatching. He also says the incubation is done entirely by the female, which coincides with our observation on the study area.

THE DESERTION OF THE DRAKES

When do the drakes abandon the sitting female? The dates when the first male concentrations were seen on the study area were noted from 1946 through 1949. The earliest was May 12, and the average was May 21. As the first brood appeared five days before this, it seems probable that the drake stays with the female during most of the incubation period and leaves for the pre-moulting concentrations only when the clutch is about to hatch. As noted previously, however, the maximum time a drake was observed to occupy the same territory was 13 days. This suggests that the use of more than one territory is the rule rather than the exception.

A measure of the number of brooding females in any specific area might be ascertained by counting the number of males in the moulting parties if they remained in the same locality. However, this does not appear to be the case on the study area. They wander about the country in groups until the actual time to moult the primaries arrives, then they are flightless for the 10 days (approximate) that it takes for the new flight feathers to develop.

FOOD DURING THE NESTING PERIOD

What food is eaten at this time? The feeding zone during the nesting period is at the edge of the retreating flood waters. From the high point of peak flood at the rear of the cultivated bottomland fields, and at the edge of the valley behind the timbered swamps, the water recedes across the fields and through the swamps, and as it drops the vegetation of these areas emerges and becomes available to the waterfowl.

The stomach of an adult male Black Duck collected on April 21 on Portobello Creek on the study area contained 9 per cent gravel, 2 per cent the bivalve mollusk *Sphaerium*, and 89 per cent seeds of *Carex, Polygonum hydropiper, Sparganium*, and unidentified shreds of vegetable matter. All of the seeds were from the previous year and were picked up at the edge of the flood. This is the typical feeding pattern at this time for both males and females.

ACCIDENTAL MORTALITY IN THE NESTING PERIOD

What natural hazards take their toll at the nest? The greatest single source of accidental mortality to nesting ducks in this region is spring muskrat trapping, but the loss of nests by flooding may be very serious in some years. The degree of seriousness of this factor depends upon the date of the peak flood. Generally speaking the later the peak flood occurs the more damage it does to nesting ducks. If the flood peaks early in the nesting period most of the nests are built above it, but if it peaks after nesting has been underway for some time, many nests will have been built either too low in the trees, or on land which will be flooded.

Flood losses occur early enough in the season in most years so that renesting almost always takes place, but as renesting clutches generally are smaller than first clutches, there probably is a loss in annual production.

Nests also are lost to forest fires, which may account for a considerable number each year. On June 24, 1947, I was flying over the upper Romaine River on the north shore of the Gulf of St. Lawrence. A large forest fire was observed burning to the barren hilltops on either side of the valley of the river. There was still snow on the ground on the north slopes and pan ice was floating in some of the lakes near the height of land, so that break-up had not long passed. Nesting was underway, and no nests in that valley would escape the flames as the fire was burning on both sides from timberline to the river and on the river islands. Some of these fires are caused by the carelessness of the Indians on their way out to the posts in the spring, and some are caused by lightning. In southern Canada, the area burned over annually is growing less year by year as modern forest protection methods are put into force, but it is significant, however, that 54.5 per cent of all forest fires occurring in New Brunswick between 1938-1946 were in the months of April, May, and June, the nesting period of Black Ducks. Nevertheless, it should be noted that these spring fires accounted for only 12.1 per cent of the total acreage burned (10). As blacks nest farther in the woods than any other ground-nesting duck, it is likely that this limiting factor is of greater significance to them than to the other local breeding species.

Predation During the Nesting Period

Who are the nest robbers? Of the seven cases of Black Duck nest predation recorded on the study area, four were attributed to raccoons, two to crows, and one to a fox. The raccoons are particularly destructive to tree nests. The Black Duck's habit of nesting in widely scattered places makes it fairly safe from excessive losses from nest predation; yet in some of the northern areas these losses may be fairly high. In northern Labrador, polar bears feed on the eggs and young of the waterfowl as a major part of their summer diet, especially in the vicinity of Davis Inlet, Nain, and Hawke's Bay (40).

An interesting ecological relationship between the nesting success of waterfowl in a certain area and the Newfoundland sealing industry was related by a fur buyer on the North Shore. When the sealing ships find a herd of seals hauled out on the floating ice, the sealers land on the ice and slaughter them for their pelts. The carcasses are left on the ice and immediately attract polar bears and Arctic foxes in great numbers. These scavangers stay with the carcasses until the last shred of food is consumed. By this time the ice pan upon which the carcasses are lying may have become detached from the main icefield and be drifting with the current.

This does not imprison the polar bears as they can and do readily swim long distances, but the foxes are stranded. If this period lasts long enough the foxes become ravenous, and if the floe does not touch another or ground on land so they can escape, they eventually will starve or drown as the ice floats southward and melts. If, however, the floe grounds on the coast of Labrador, Newfoundland, or the North Shore, a horde of ravenous foxes is loosed on the country immediately surrounding the point of contact with land, and every living thing small enough for them to kill is devoured quickly. They may wipe out the nesting population of waterfowl in the vicinity as they will eat both eggs and adults, and will clean out renesting attempts as fast as they are made if they cannot catch the females. The concentration soon disperses as they spread out over the country, but the damage to nesting waterfowl may have reduced the production of that area drastically for the season. This is said to have happened on several occasions in Labrador and on the North Shore.

Human destruction of nesting ducks in this region does not appear to be serious. The Indians of the Maritime Provinces, the Micmacs and Maliceets, are too civilized today to do much nest hunting for eggs. They spend considerable time during the nesting season in the bottomlands gathering "fiddleheads," edible ferns which they sell on the market, and they may find some nests at this time. If they rob them it is done on the spur of the moment and not as a common practice.

The Indians of Newfoundland are extinct, but the average Newfoundlander of the outports shoots seabirds for food and will take and eat any eggs he can find. In Labrador, occasional egging raids still are made on the seabird rookeries by the fishing schooners lying off shore. This practice has little effect upon the fresh-water ducks as they are then on the inland waters. The Indians of the North Shore are the Montagnais and are typical fur hunters. They spend their summers at the posts on the coast, and as the nesting waterfowl are in the interior, they do not have the opportunity to do much damage.

In northern Labrador and Ungava the Indians are the Nascaupees, the most primitive tribe in the east. They are very few in number and spend the summer at the posts on the Atlantic coast, at Fort McKenzie on the Kaniapiskau, or at Fort Chimo where that river changes its name to the Eskimo word *Koksoak*. The Fort Chimo band numbered only about 25 tents at the time of our visit in 1948. The men spend their time lying around the post, and the women and children pick berries on the barrens within a three-mile radius. As the vicinity of Fort Chimo is not duck nesting habitat, they do no damage to waterfowl.

The Ungava Eskimos living north of the trees on the mainland of Quebec and Labrador are in a position to do more damage than the Indians. The Quebec population numbered 2,100 in 1944. As mentioned previously, this is a population density of one Eskimo to every 43 square miles and two miles of coast, and is a higher density than that of the rest of the Eastern Arctic. These people rob every nest they find, but I have not heard of their doing so in a systematic manner. Their dogs likewise are very destructive of any wildlife in the vicinity of their camps, but as they usually are chained at this season the damage is small. They are mostly a boat people during the summer, and do not travel far inland; so their effect on the annual waterfowl production of the vast region in which they live must be small indeed. They travel by "peterhead" boat around the shores of Ungava Bay, where the tides are among the strongest in the world, and lie up each low tide wherever they happen to be stranded and hunt the surrounding country for anything alive "until the sea comes back."

It should be remembered, however, that the Indian name for the Whale River in Ungava Bay was *Manouan,* or "the egg-gathering place" (Cabot in 40). We do not know what kind of eggs were gathered there, but they probably were eider eggs as these ducks were abundant on the coast, and their method of nesting makes them most vulnerable to the egg hunter. The scattered nesting of blacks would hardly earn the locality such a name.

Another good reason why the northern natives do not hunt duck nests extensively is that the ducks are nesting at the time they are catching up on the year's social activities. The buryings, marryings, baptizings, and courtings of the year have to be attended to at this time, and it is the first opportunity to eat "store food" in quantity for many a long month; so nobody is interested in hunting seriously for widely scattered duck nests. Colony-nesting species such as the eiders would, however, not have this disadvantage from the point of view of the natives, and those colonies situated near a post no doubt are raided.

Chapter III

Life in the Creeks and Ponds

THE BROOD season on the study area in New Brunswick usually starts, within two days more or less, on May 16. One of the favorite places for watching broods making their way out of the woods and into the streams and flood waters is a road running through a 15-year-old burn behind the village of Upper Gagetown. The road runs at right angles to the main river, and each year at this time Black Duck broods are found walking and swimming down the ditch of the roadside toward the river. They are found more than two miles into the burn, which is now a jungle of very dense wire birch and aspen 10 to 20 feet high.

The spring run-off has filled every hollow at the time the females are building their nests; so they are placed on top of hummocks in clumps of *Spiraea* or bracken, and are well covered by the developing foliage of the birch-aspen reproduction on the burn. In the latter part of May the road through the burn becomes a flowing brook down which the ducklings

45

swim to the primary rearing covers in the alder-lined creeks and sloughs, but by June 1 it dries up, and then the ducklings make the two-mile journey on foot and hence are vulnerable to predators.

Primary Rearing Cover

Where do the ducklings spend their first two weeks? Primary rearing cover is that used by the brood in the first two weeks of its life. The female chooses the most dense alder-lined creeks, streams, and ponds where abundant escape cover always is at hand. The main food of the ducklings at this time is insects, and these thickly overgrown areas abound in this type of food. Surface foods are preferred as the young do not tip up or dive, and areas where the food is several inches under water are of little use to young ducklings. Inland marshes are practically non-existent in this region at the time the first broods hatch, as last year's emergent aquatics still are submerged and this year's growth is just beginning. What will be a marsh in July is an open lake with no food or cover in May and early June, and it is of no use to small broods.

The coastwise nesting Black Ducks use the tidal stream estuaries as primary rearing cover. Insect foods are abundant there, but escape cover consists of the thick salt marsh grasses rather than the alder fringe of the inland streams.

The ducklings stay in the primary rearing cover until they have passed the downy stage and are growing their first feathers. By this time the flood waters have receded, and the areas which will be marshes for the rest of the season are beginning to show above water. The hen then leads her brood out of the alders and into the open marshes, where they are easy to see until the emergent vegetation has developed sufficiently to hide them once again.

Secondary Rearing Cover

Where do the young ducks live until fully feathered? The secondary rearing cover is the habitat in which the ducklings will live from the time they have grown their first feathers until they are able to fly. It is the marshes and lake shores of the interior and the mud flats and reefs of the coast. Here the ducklings grow rapidly for five or six weeks, and at the end of their eighth week of life they are ready to start their first short flights.

In the interior the marsh vegetation has developed rapidly, and once again abundant escape cover is on every hand. The ducklings have learned to eat seeds and other vegetable foods and have now forsaken the insect diet of their first two weeks. The food of the adults and young is essentially the same now and consists of about 80 per cent vegetable foods and 20 per cent animal food, consisting mainly of snails and insects for the birds in the fresh-water habitats.

HATCHING SUCCESS AND BROOD SURVIVAL

How many eggs hatch and how many ducklings reach flying age? The hatching success and brood survival of Black Ducks and the other local nesting species have been followed on the study area from 1945-1949. The year 1949 is compared with the average of the years 1945-1949. This is a full five-year average for Black Ducks, but for some of the other species no data were obtained in one or more years, and the actual number of years used for each species is shown in the table.

The average sizes of the different classes of broods of Black Ducks were computed from a count of 259 broods containing 1,826 ducklings. The numbers used in the computations for the other species are smaller in proportion to their abundance on the study area. It will be seen that the average brood of Black Ducks less than two weeks old is eight, and in the nesting study the average completed clutch was found to be nine. This suggests that infertile eggs may be responsible for a loss of one egg, or 11 per cent of the clutch.

A further 19 per cent of the original clutch is lost through predation and accidental mortality by the time the ducklings are three-quarters grown. The rise in brood size after the ducklings are six weeks or over in age can be accounted for

TABLE I. HATCHING SUCCESS AND BROOD
SURVIVAL

Study Area, N. B.

Species	Before reaching water		CLASS I		CLASS II		CLASS III		REMARKS
	Broods	Dkls/ Brood	No. Broods	Dkls/ Brood	No. Broods	Dkls/ Brood	No. Broods	Dkls/ Brood	
Black Duck									
Avr (45-49)	....	....	23.2	8.0	12.4	5.7	16.2	6.3	
1949	5	10.0	43	7.1	30	5.5	51	6.6	
B. W. Teal									
Avr (45-49)	....	....	1.4	6.3	3.2	5.5	°4.5	°7.1	°4 yrs.
1949	....	....	1	5.0	8	6.2	4	8.0	
G. W. Teal									
Avr (45-49)	....	....	2.4	5.5	2.4	6.1	°5.0	°5.8	°2 yrs.
1949	....	....	3	5.0	3	6.0	5	5.6	
Wood Duck									
Avr (45-49)	....	....	°8.2	°5.6	9.4	5.7	8.0	6.5	°4 yrs.
1949	....	....	18	5.5	28	5.2	20	5.6	
Ring-Necked Duck									
Avr (45-49)	....	....	24.6	6.6	16.4	6.4	°8.7	°6.0	°4 yrs.
1949	....	....	39	6.6	20	5.7	18	5.3	
Am. Golden-eye									
Avr (45-49)	....	....	°28.0	°6.2	10.6	4.3	9.0	5.0	°4 yrs.
1949	....	....	35	5.3	15	3.9	11	4.4	

Size/Age Classes:

Class   I = up to ¼ grown, i.e. in the down; up to 2 weeks.
Class   II = ¼-¾ grown; 2 weeks-6 weeks.
Class III = ¾ grown to awing; 6 weeks-8 weeks.

only by the practice of accumulation of ducklings which is known to take place in almost all species, and it is shown here for all species except greenwings and ringnecks. When a female deserts a brood to moult before the young can fly they usually join the first brood they encounter. This accounts for instances when ducklings of two different age groups are found in a single brood.

An important check on the brood counts in New Brunswick is provided by the tabulation of 487,499 broods counted in the Prairie Provinces by Ducks Unlimited in the years 1935, 1938-43. This tremendous amount of data, from almost three million ducks, showed that both diving ducks and fresh-water ducks average six ducklings per brood in late July in the Canadian west in all years (22, and personal communications for 1943 data). It was particularly interesting to find in this compilation a count of 123 broods of Black Ducks made in Manitoba, the western limit of the breeding range. These western breeders averaged 6.4 ducklings per brood in the five years 1938-43 (excluding 1941). As the New Brunswick counts averaged 6.3 ducklings per brood at the same age between 1945-49, it would seem from these data that there is no appreciable difference in brood survival between east and west, although the causes of mortality may be quite different. It is noted, however, that Bennett (12) found only five young reaching the migratory stage in the Blue-winged Teal in Iowa.

It appears, therefore, that of the original clutch of nine eggs, one fails to hatch, and an additional 1.7 ducklings are killed before the survivors reach the age of six weeks. As the broods then accumlate 0.6 ducklings before they are awing, a certain number of broods must break up, and the total number of broods reaching the flying stage must be smaller than the number at the half-grown stage. This does not appear in the table for a number of reasons, such as the relative difficulty of finding large and small ducklings, and the difference in the state of development of the aquatic vegetation early and late in the season which makes the finding of broods easier in the early season.

DUCKLING MORTALITY FACTORS

Disease and Parasites. The most serious cause of duckling mortality from disease and parasites among Black Ducks is the protozoan blood parasite *Leucocytozoon anatis,* Wickware. This parasite causes a disease in young ducks similar to malaria. It is transmitted from duck to duck by the bite of its alterna-

tive host, the blackfly, and has caused serious mortality among
young Black Ducks in Michigan. Its life history and method
of transmission were described by O'Roke (88), who con-
siders that it is responsible for heavy mortality among wild
ducks.

He found that mortality was heaviest among ducklings that
were small during the height of the blackfly season, and less
severe in those which had grown to considerable size before
the peak of the fly season, or had hatched after the peak had
passed. The geographical distribution of the disease is known
to cover large irregular districts in Michigan and other parts of
the United States. As blackflies are common over the northern
breeding grounds, it seems probable that the disease is fairly
widespread. There is as yet no means of estimating the seriousness of the loss due to this parasite, and O'Roke's results
showed that mortality in ducklings varied from 10 to 100
per cent, and was less than 1 per cent for adults.

The asexual stage of the life cycle of the parasite occurs in
the duck and requires 10 days, and the sexual stage in the
fly requires 2 to 5 days. The parasite was found in ducks the
year round, but in winter it inhabits the interior organs and
only in summer is it found in the blood stream where it is
available to the blackflies. No practical means of controlling
the disease in wild populations have been developed yet.

Blood slides were collected on the study area from 30 ducks.
Nineteen were Black Ducks and two were adults; the others
were young, ranging in age from one week to six months.
The gametocyte stage of the parasite was found in the blood
of three of the young blacks, but external evidence of the
disease was not noted in these birds, and they appeared normal
in every respect. The maximum infestation was four per field,
and 31 per half hour of searching under 20X magnification.

Microfilaria were found in six of the 19 blacks, two of the
six ringnecks, and one of the five goldeneyes. The type found
closely resembled Nelson and Gashwiler's (5) Type A, 45-65
microns long and 4-6 microns in diameter with a short curved
tail. Adult worms were not found, and the maximum infestation was eight per field of 0.61 mm. diameter.

Plate XVIII. At low tide in Ungava Bay the peterhead boats of the Eskimo lie up wherever they happen to be and the owners hunt the surrounding barrens for anything alive "until the sea comes back."

Photo by W. H. Carrick

Plate XIX. Newly hatched ducklings about to leave the nest.

Plate **XX**. The Primary Rearing Cover of the interior is the alder-lined creeks and streams where the ducklings spend the first two weeks of their lives. On the coast it is the estuaries of the tidal streams running through the salt marshes.

Plate XXI. The Secondary Rearing Cover of the interior. The Grand Lake marshes of New Brunswick with a brood of pen-reared Mallards in the foreground just after their release.

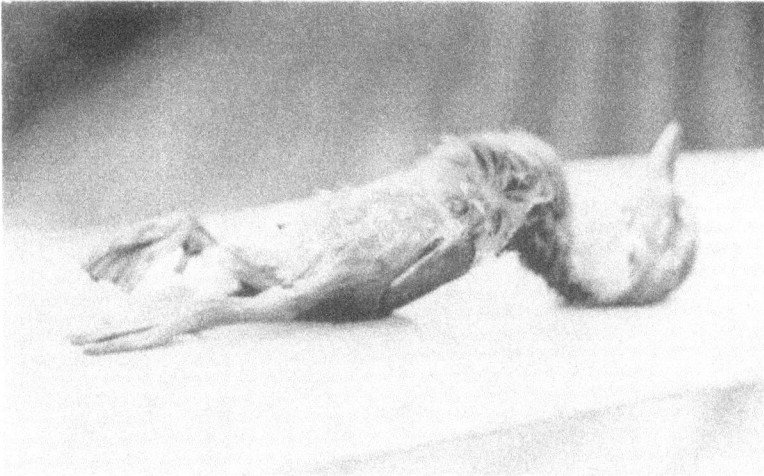

Photo by A. Gordon

Plate XXII. Black Duck duckling killed by an unidentified fish. It was pulled underwater, bitten, and released to float to the surface in a dying condition.

Photo by A. W. Skead

Plate XXIII. Trout large enough to be duckling predators abound in the northern lakes. They may be a factor in brood survival.

Plate XXIV. Cap Tourmente on the St. Lawrence, a famous assembly point for blacks, and the only region where the Greater Snow Goose can be hunted in southeastern Canada.

Photo by A. J. Reeve

Plate XXV. An assembly point on the Labrador coast, the salt marshes at Tinker Harbour at the mouth of Hamilton Inlet where a banding station was established.

No sick ducks were found in the five field seasons of the study so it appears that, while the parasite is present, it is not a serious mortality factor in this region.

Botulism usually is regarded as a disease of the alkaline ponds of the west, but it recently has been reported from the Susquehanna River, which is a noted wintering ground for blacks, and five dead birds and one sick one were found there in the fall of 1949. The disease that killed these blacks was diagnosed definitely as botulism, but there is little cause for anxiety that it will spread through the eastern breeding grounds as the acid waters of the northeast would act as a deterrent to the spread of the bacterium. Cold weather during the migration, and the natural aeration of lakes by springs and streams, also make unfavorable conditions for it.

This study has uncovered no evidence that disease and parasites were serious causes of mortality to ducklings in this region during the five years 1945-1949.

Predation. The total loss of ducklings through accidental mortality, disease, parasites, and predation in the first six weeks of their lives is shown by the brood survival data to be about 21 per cent. We have been unable to attribute any cases of duckling mortality to accidents, or directly to disease and parasites, so it appears that most of this loss is due to predation.

Eight cases of duckling predation were observed in the course of the study. Two kills were made by Bald Eagles, one by a Marsh Hawk and one by a Red-tailed Hawk. One kill was made by a fox, and two were attributed to snapping turtles. One kill only was attributed to a pickerel or an eel.

A study of pickerel predation was made in 1948 under a grant from the Associate Committee on Wildlife Research of the National Research Council of Canada, and 367 pickerel were netted in the study area during the brood season. Of these only 59 contained prey remains, 58 of which were fish and one was an insect (140). There is no doubt, however, that pickerel and/or eels do take ducklings in the areas since on June 20, 1949, a downy young Black Duck was pulled under before our eyes, bitten, and released in a dying condition by an unseen fish. This duckling is shown in Plate XXII.

The abundance of large and voracious eels in the St. John estuary gives reason to suspect that they may be duckling predators of some importance. Several instances of their having attacked wounded ducks floating in front of a blind are on record, but we have not been able to prove that they take ducklings. On one occasion a three-quarter grown Wood Duck became entangled in the top of the pickerel net and was devoured by eels within a few hours. This duck was a captive in the net, however, and not free to escape the attack of the eels.

The presence of snapping turtles on the area was indicated by two ducklings found with the end of the beak and one leg bitten off respectively. The stump of the leg was healed already although the duckling still was in the downy stage. Several types of turtle traps were set in the study area but without result. From this it was concluded that, if they were present at all, they were not numerous.

A study of the food habits of the Bald Eagles summering in the estuary also was made in 1949-1950 under a grant from the Associate Committee on Wildlife Research of the National Research Council of Canada. Of 138 eagle meals examined, only 6 per cent were uninjured ducks (141). The estuary of the St. John is a concentration point for the eagles summering in the Maritime Provinces, and the peak population is reached by August 1. After this date they start south, and by mid-September there are only a few left. It is significant that at the time of the maximum build-up of the waterfowl population in late summer and early fall the eagles have left the area, showing that their preference for waterfowl as food is low at this time. Coarse fish of 8 species make up 40 per cent of their food during their stay in the estuary so that they are not a serious predator on breeding ducks, although an individual eagle may form this habit.

Upon several occasions, broods of ducks were seen to swim directly under a Bald Eagle sitting on an overhanging branch, and, although both appeared to see the other, the ducks showed no alarm and the eagle paid no attention to them. After the freeze-up, however, the picture seems to change as fish food becomes unavailable, and the eagle must rely more upon birds and mammals. This is predation on adults, however, and not ducklings, and will be taken up in a later section.

Downy young Black Ducks are taken by bullfrogs in the Ottawa River (52), and since large bullfrogs are common in the St. John estuary, it is likely that they also are an occasional predator there.

In the northern breeding grounds the fox and the raven, the mink and the Great Black-backed Gull, the Great Horned Owl and the lynx must be considered as possible duckling predators. The lakes contain large trout and northern pike, and bass in the southern areas, and these too are potential enemies of young ducks. Large lake trout and a ling-like fish, the cusk (called the "morai" in Labrador), are to be found in the lakes of Ungava, but no one knows if they are duckling predators, although they grow to a size that would make a young Black Duck an ordinary mouthful.

Despite this rather lengthy list of possible enemies there is no evidence of excessive predation on young Black Ducks, and the losses that are suffered can be attributed to a number of species. In fact, with the exception of the snowshoe rabbit, the beaver, and the muskrat, all the fur animals of the north are potential duck predators, and their production on an area is of considerably greater value to the local inhabitants than that of waterfowl. Therefore, any suggestion of predator control for the benefit of waterfowl would be considered favoring a secondary group of species at the expense of a primary one; in other words, waterfowl are a good fur food. For this reason predator control measures would receive short shrift in those areas which still are dependent largely on the fur trade. We even had difficulty in disposing of muskrats caught in our banding traps on the North Shore of the Gulf of St. Lawrence without offending the local inhabitants. Cases of mink robbing duck traps had to be dealt with in all possible secrecy because each animal destroyed was considered a direct monetary loss by the local trappers.

In summarizing the mortality factors of young Black Ducks, we find that of the original clutch of nine eggs, one fails to hatch. Within the next six to eight weeks 1.7 ducklings are killed by a combination of accidents, disease and parasites, and predation. Of these three, predation seems to be the most serious on the area studied, but no particular species is outstanding as a duckling predator. Thus 6.3 ducklings reach the flying stage and pass out of the stage of maximum vulnerability to predation into the adult category, where the number of possible predators is considerably smaller.

Chapter IV

Awing & Away!

THE FEMALES AND YOUNG IN LATE SUMMER

THE YOUNG usually make their first short flights in their eighth week and are then deserted by the female. They stay together as a brood for a few days, but soon they mix with other broods and form gangs of 10 to 20, trading about the marshes. Their flight at this time is characterized by a much more rapid wing-beat than that of the adults, and they seem to be working much harder, so that the young of the year can be identified in the air by a practiced eye even when there is no available scale against which to judge their size. They rapidly gain in flying skill and confidence and make longer and longer journeys, and it is at this time that Black Ducks are reported on the prairies many hundreds of miles west of the nearest known breeding grounds. Three immature males were banded near Brooks, Alberta, on September 8, 1943, and, as far as is known, the species does not breed in Canada west of the extreme eastern edge of Manitoba.

The young birds soon find the concentrations of moulting males that have been wandering about the marshes since early summer and join them. Through binoculars they can be distinguished from the adult males by their much smaller size and their olive-drab bills and feet, but it is easy to confuse them with some of the early nesting females that have completed their moult and have joined the males by mid-August.

It is at these assembly points that the young first see their fathers and begin to learn some of the caution that has enabled individuals of their species to run the gauntlet of gunfire each fall, stretching from the northern breeding grounds to the winter range, as many as 17 times. Many do not learn in time, however, and the kill on "opening day" each year contains a large proportion of young birds.

Certain points in the country are used year after year as assembly points for the Black Duck flights. The west end of the Island of Orleans north channel in the St. Lawrence is one such point. There moulting adults and flying young from the surrounding lakes, streams, and marshes can be seen each August resting on the boulders at low tide, or rafted out in the channel during daylight as summer merges into fall. The wily old males begin to assume their hunting-season feeding pattern of going ashore only after dark to feed and spending the dangerous daylight hours rafted in open water where they cannot be approached.

The lagoon in Musquash Island in the St. John estuary in New Brunswick is another assembly point. Blacks and ringnecks use this sheltered lagoon in large numbers, and they have found it a safe haven even during the hunting season as they are out of range of blinds on shore and have plenty of room to circle to a safe altitude before crossing land if they are flushed by a boat.

When the females desert their broods, they hide in the densest part of the marsh to moult. They do not come together in numbers as the males do, but prefer to keep to themselves. If, however, there is only one suitable moulting cover available, considerable numbers may use the same marsh, but if you would see them, each must be hunted separately as there is no massed flushing as with a gang of males.

The first broods of the season are deserted by the females in southern New Brunswick about July 11. Moulting females may be found in the marshes from that date to at least September 15. A few years ago the hunting season opened in New Brunswick on September 15, and it was not an uncommon practice to send the dogs out to collect "flappers." A few of those "flappers" were of late broods still unable to fly, but most were adult females still flightless in moult. This practice has been abolished by opening the season on October 1, and by that date there are no "flappers" left on the marsh.

At the extreme northern edge of the breeding range the flightless period of the females extends almost to the first freeze, since on August 25th I collected two that were flightless and one with very new primaries in a pool on the rocky dry barrens at False River, Ungava Bay. The shorebird migration was in full swing by that date, and the pools in the barrens freeze at night in early September, so those ducks must start south as soon as the primaries are formed.

It is interesting to note that Mr. Bob May of George River Post is convinced that blacks do not breed at Ungava Bay as he never has seen young in his travels over the surrounding country. On our trip in this country in August and September, 1948, we counted and estimated 2,153 ducks and geese in the period August 16-26. Of these 1,735, or 81 per cent were blacks. Neither Dr. Gabrielson nor I saw a bird we could identify as a young Black Duck, and of the eight specimens I was able to collect, five were males and three females, and all were adults.

It would seem, therefore, that there is evidence that the blacks summering in Ungava Bay are moulting males and non-breeding females, and that the mates of the males raise their broods in the taiga south of the barrens. Three Indian hunters of the Kaniapiskau—Shamani and Chescapio, both Nascaupees, and John Nattawapio, a Cree—told me that they have seen downy young blacks on the upper reaches of that river, but never in the barrenlands. Conversely, Johnny Angnetuk, our Eskimo skipper and guide, who had spent his life on the tidewaters of Ungava Bay, could not recall having seen young *me-tuk-luks,* the Eskimo name for Black Ducks.

Flying young are not averse to traveling north in the late summer, and it is difficult to understand why they do not go to the nearest salt water as they do elsewhere. There is as yet insufficient evidence to prove that they do not, and the solution of this point must await further fieldwork. It is significant, however, that neither Turner (132), Eklund and Cool (27), Hildebrand (54), nor Gabrielson and Wright (36) were able to provide proof of Black Ducks breeding on the shores of Ungava Bay, and for the latter observers the solution of this point was one of the main objectives of the trip.

The Life of the Males in Summer and Early Autumn

The earliest observed date of a male concentration in southern New Brunswick was May 12, and the average was May 21. On June 23 the earliest record of a flightless black was made when one was killed crossing the highway. The male concentrations usually appear about the date the first broods are seen, and at this time they are fairly small, numbering between 20 and 50. They do not stay in one marsh but wander over the country wherever there is suitable habitat, and for this reason counts of flightless males or of male concentrations cannot be used to determine breeding populations on any given marsh. There were no moulting males on our study area in New Brunswick in the summer of 1946, but in the next four seasons many were found.

As the time to moult the primaries approaches, the males become more and more localized, and then they usually are found in the largest marshes in the county. The actual flightless period lasts about 10 days, during which they are secretive and become expert at hiding in holes and clumps of marsh vegetation when chased. If pursued in the water they will dive readily, but they will always make for shore to hide in

the grass and will not head for the center of the lake as will the divers. It is possible to catch them for banding at this time by the use of a well- trained and light-mouthed retriever, but without a really first-class dog this method is not recommended as too many birds will be injured if they are handled roughly by the dog.

When the new primaries are formed the males move to the assembly points where they are joined soon by the first flying young and a little later by the first of the adult females to complete their family duties for the year. There is some evidence, already given, that these adult females pair off again very soon after joining the males, but whether this is temporary or permanent pairing it is not possible to say.

The gathering at the assembly point at Musquash Island lagoon in the St. John estuary in New Brunswick builds up to about 1,000 birds by the 15th of September, and about half of these are ringnecks. Other important assembly points in the Maritime Provinces are the Missiquash-Tantramar Marshes on the New Brunswick-Nova Scotia border, and Pisguid Pond in Prince Edward Island.

There are many assembly points along the St. Lawrence, but some of the principal ones are in the western end and along the south shore of Lake St. Peter, in the north channel of the Island of Orleans, and at the Seal Islands about 20 miles downriver from the eastern end of the island. On the Labrador coast a favorite assembly point is Tinker Harbour on the south shore of Hamilton Inlet, and in Ungava Bay it is the tidal meadows at the mouth of False River. In Newfoundland, the mouth of the Grand Codroy River in the extreme southwest corner is used by both local birds and migrants.

In their wanderings, both before and after they become flightless, adults of both sexes have appeared in the far west. Houston (57) reports two adult males banded at Leach Lake, Saskatchewan. One was banded on July 21, 1945, presumably before moulting its primaries, and the other on October 17 after the annual moults are over and the bird is in fall plumage. Two adult females, one flightless, were banded at Rousay Lake, Saskatchewan, on August 10 and 22 respectively. Both were shot in November far to the east, one in Ontario and the other in Illinois. As there was no evidence of a brood it is presumed that these were non-breeding females, or at least that they did not breed that year. Two adult males and an adult female were banded near Yorktown, Saskatchewan, also in 1945, and by mid-summer the species is distributed widely in small groups over most of Manitoba. Three immature males were banded near Brooks, Alberta, in 1943, and a specimen was collected in the Athabaska Delta in 1940.

The Blue-winged Teal join the concentrations of blacks along the St. Lawrence and in the Maritimes, but they do not stay long. They are the first to start south before there is any sign of severe weather, and the peak of their migration has passed before gunning starts in southern Canada. Ringnecks, goldeneyes, Green-winged Teal, and Wood Ducks are present at the assembly points in the Maritimes, but farther north the goldeneyes and Wood Ducks are replaced largely by Pintails. Greenwings are abundant along the north shore of the Gulf of St. Lawrence, but they are surpassed in numbers by the Pintails along the Labrador coast and in Ungava. Along the entire coastline from Hudson Strait to the St. Lawrence, the blacks have large numbers of eiders and scoters sharing the offshore ledges with them. These species act in many places as buffers for the blacks, as they are approached and shot more easily by the natives.

At this time of year there is no evidence of loss from disease such as occurs frequently in the West when botulism outbreaks follow the drying up of alkaline ponds. This dread disease does come east occasionally, however, as in September and October, 1949, two widely separated outbreaks, which killed a few Black Ducks, were reported in Pennsylvania.

Lead poisoning is another source of mortality which so far has not been reported in this region. Predation takes place, but it is not excessive, and what losses do occur can be attributed to a number of species. No one predator makes a practice of hunting Black Ducks, and at this time of year they are found in large bodies of water and extensive marshes where the number of possible predators is limited.

Chapter V

The Time of Scarlet and Gold

THE FALL MIGRATION

As THE long days of late summer begin to
shorten, and scarlet and gold creep over the hills of eastern
Canada, the blacks in the center of the Labrador-Ungava
country start to move to the coast. Some of the great lakes of
the interior are more than 500 square miles in area, and, as
previously mentioned, trappers at North West River say they
find large rafts of ducks and Canada geese on these lakes when
they are on their way to their traplines in the fall. These

63

presumably are concentrations of birds which have been in the interior all summer, or perhaps overland migrants from Ungava Bay to the Gulf of St. Lawrence.

The young of the year lead the southward movement, and this in itself suggests that they do not need the guidance of the adults. The movement is not a steady journey to the wintering grounds, but rather a series of southward moves to get out of areas of unfavorable weather. They move on to a new locality and stay there until frozen out, or until all the choice food is consumed, and it is this matter of choice foods which is of great importance in determining the areas that will hold Black Ducks in the fall.

Little is known about the foods of the Black Duck in the region between the Maine border and Ungava Bay. We collected 59 stomachs between July 25 and December 29 in this region, and the results of their analyses are shown in Appendix III. Table II shows the percentage of animal and vegetable foods consumed at five collecting stations scattered from the Bay of Fundy to Ungava Bay. All stomachs were collected during the period of late summer concentrations and fall migration.

Specimens were collected at the assembly point at False River on the south shore of Ungava Bay. The most widely used waterfowl food of this area in late summer is the Crowberry, *Empetrum nigrum.* This berry was found in 6 of the 8 Black Ducks collected, 6 of the 13 Pintails, 8 of the 9 greenwings, in both of the 2 Old Squaws, and in 1 of the 2 Redbreasted Mergansers. It was not found in the 1 American Goldeneye collected, nor in either of the 2 Canada Geese. A larger sample of geese probably would have shown the berry to be utilized, as they were seen grazing among the plants. It made up 47 per cent by volume of the food in the Black Ducks. The most important animal food was snails, probably *Littoria obstusata,* with amphipods and Cladocera making up the balance.

This area is a tidal estuary, and the greater part of the waterfowl were found on salt water. However, they resorted

TABLE II. BLACK DUCK FOODS: LATE SUMMER AND FALL, UNGAVA TO MAINE

Collecting Station	No. Stomachs	Per Cent of Total Veg.	Animal	Dates Collected
False River, Ungava	8	65	35	Aug. 23-26
Tinker Harbor, Labrador ...	10	55	45	Aug. 17—Sept. 22
Baie Johan Beetz, Quebec ...	14	76	20	Aug. 13—Oct. 20
St. John Valley, New Brunswick	23	92	5	July 23—Oct. 8
Bay of Fundy, N. B. —Maine Border	4	Tr.	100	Dec. 19-29
Total	59	..	..	
Average	..	59	41	

to the salt meadows to feed where they consumed the available vegetable food in preference to the abundant supply of snails and marine algae on the tide flats. Even the divers frequented the tundra pools and ate crowberries, as is shown by the occurrence of this berry in Old Squaws and Red-breasted Mergansers.

At Tinker Harbor on the Labrador coast, at the mouth of Hamilton Inlet, the habitat is again an area of tidal creeks and ponds extending back into the scrub and muskeg. Here the vegetable foods also were preferred to animal foods, and crowberry again was utilized, although not as extensively as in Ungava Bay. The animal foods were again snails and amphipods.

At Baie Johan Beetz on the North Shore of the Gulf of St. Lawrence, the blacks showed a distinct preference for fresh-water vegetable foods although they spend the greater part of the day on salt water. The Cowlily, *Nuphar rubrodisca*, was the most important fresh-water species utilized in that region.

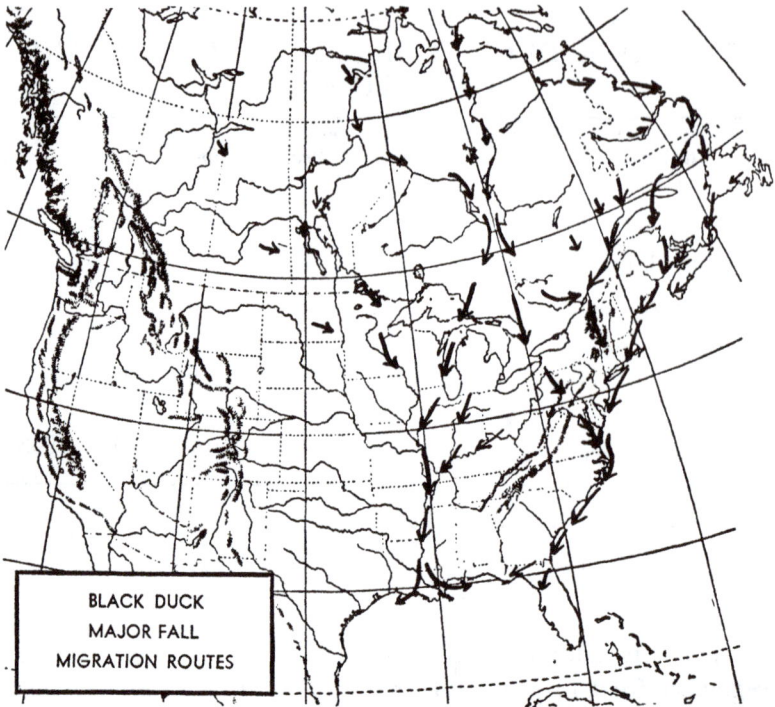

BLACK DUCK
MAJOR FALL
MIGRATION ROUTES

An interesting observation was made there on the versatility of the feeding habits of the species. Kutz (61) demonstrated that Black Ducks will dive for food in water up to 10 feet deep. His experiments were conducted under artificial conditions, however, and there is no record in the literature of this having been observed in the field. On October 31, 1948, at Victor Bay, Saguenay County, Quebec, a number of Black Ducks were observed diving for food by Andrew W. Skead who was operating the banding station at Baie Johan Beetz. He collected a specimen from among the diving birds, and its stomach contained eelgrass, salt-water snails, and bivalve mollusks (*Pelecypoda*). The specimen collected was an adult male, and it had been feeding in salt water about 12 feet deep with a heavy surf running. There were 18 birds in the group, and they were watched for 20 minutes at short range. Skead described their actions as similar to that of American Goldeneyes, with which he was very familiar.

On the 31st October, 1953, I was calling moose beside a small beaver pond on the extreme headwaters of the Nipisiquit River in New Brunswick. My guide and I had heard ducks pass overhead in the fog on our way to the pond, and when we got there a pair of Black Ducks emerged from the early morning shadows on the far side and swam out into the center. We stayed out of sight and gave a call on the birchbark moose horn, which did not disturb them in the least, and they both began diving for food. There were no aquatics showing on the surface, and as the dam had been breached recently the shoreline was an empty mudflat, so the only food available for ducks in the pond was on the bottom. They dived with the same forward plunge of a goldeneye, but with a noticeable splash each time. They stayed submerged for 10 to 15 seconds, and rose and flapped their wings each time they returned to the surface.

They were less than 30 yards away and were observed through 10 X binoculars for more than a half hour. They brought to the surface strings of what appeared to be burreed which were broken up and swallowed while swimming about. On a previous visit to the pond I had seen root clumps and shreds of vegetation around the shore as if diving ducks had been feeding there, although it is a small pond in the deep forest far from any known diving duck habitat. That day's observation cleared up the mystery and showed that the Black Duck, the forest duck of the northeast, turns into a diving duck when so required.

The Black Duck flight moves westward along the north shore of the Gulf of St. Lawrence until it reaches Anticosti Island. From there the direction is south to the Gaspé Peninsula and along the north shore of New Brunswick into the Maritime Provinces. This is shown clearly in the banding returns from Baie Johan Beetz, where large numbers of Black Ducks have been banded and only a few have so far been recovered on the St. Lawrence west of Anticosti, all the others being recovered on the coastal route. The St. Lawrence flight thus comes from the watershed of the lower river and the hinterland to the north.

The Newfoundland birds congregate at the mouth of the Grand Codroy river before crossing Cabot Strait to the mainland. Some of the Labrador birds come south along the west coast of Newfoundland, and there is a small wintering population along the south coast each year.

The local-bred birds of southern New Brunswick gather in the estuary of the St. John, and in the Missiquash-Tantramar marshes on the Nova Scotia border, and they are joined by the first flights of young birds from the north. In the St. John valley they are in an exclusive fresh-water habitat once again, and the 23 stomachs collected there showed that they ate 92 per cent vegetable foods of which wildrice, *Zizania acquatica,* was the largest single item. Blacks remain in the estuary until the edges freeze over and deny them access to the marsh vegetation; then they move on to the Bay of Fundy shore.

The last to arrive from the north are large adult birds which are thought to be predominantly males. They arrive in Grand Lake in numbers toward the middle of November, when the first of the really cold weather drives them from the coastal lagoons of northern New Brunswick; it is these large adults in full winter plumage that are known all along the flyway as the "Northern Red-Legs," or "Labrador Blacks," and for many years they were considered to be a separate species. It is possible that these large adults are non-breeders which have summered in Ungava Bay, since they do not show up in the records of the northern banding stations. These stations were all closed by October 30, and a late migration would not be sampled, but they are more likely old birds that will not enter a trap. As they have been in a much colder climate for some time, they have developed their full winter plumage with bright orange feet and yellow bills in the males and mottled olive-green bills in the females before the local birds, and therefore look quite different from them.

Most of the local birds have left almost a month before the northern flight of adults arrives, having been chased out by the heavy early-season gunning, and the newcomers thus look much larger and different to the gunners.

Shortt (111) illustrates these changes in coloration, and we have found no points of divergence from his findings. One female was captured with her brood in Newfoundland before she lost the orange-red color of her legs and feet, so that we had an example of a "Northern Red-legged Black Duck" raising a brood of "Common Black Ducks" to substantiate him.

When they reach the Bay of Fundy shore they have arrived on the winter range, and for the ducks that winter in salt-water habitat the diet is mainly animal matter. One of the outstanding sources of food is the Little Blue Mussel, *Mytilus*. Various snails and periwinkles also are important.

The birds from central and western Quebec concentrate in the marshes of the St. Lawrence. These are tidal marshes from below Rimouski to the Island of Orleans and above, but at Lake St. Peter the brackish and saltwater habitats are left behind and the south shore of the lake and the western end contain some of the finest freshwater marshes in eastern Canada. Here large numbers of Black Ducks congregate and stay throughout the fall in company with Mallards and rafts of diving ducks which come from breeding grounds to the west. Lake St. Peter is a true melting-pot of species from both east and west, and it is considered to be the western limit of the eastern section of the flyway. Blacks banded in James Bay in August have been retaken in the traps in Lake St. Peter in November, showing that the St. Lawrence birds and the James Bay flight meet here. The point of entry into the United States of this population is thought to be via Lake Champlain, but a banding station has just been established on the lake, and its results will bring out this point more clearly.

The Black Ducks leave the vicinity of George River in Ungava Bay in September, but there still are a few birds

north of Hamilton Inlet on the Labrador coast by the first
week of October. By November 15, the main flight has left
the Gulf and Lower St. Lawrence region, and the last big
flights arrive in Maine before the middle of December.
Stragglers remain as far north as ice conditions permit, and
a small number winter on the south coast of Newfoundland.
The birds wintering in this extreme northern tip of the
winter range thus never enter the region of heavy gunning
and do not experience this important mortality factor.

The average dates of departure from key points in southern Canada are Ottawa, November 17, with late departures
up to the 21st; Montreal, November 6, with stragglers to the
14th; and Prince Edward Island, November 13, with stragglers
to December 8. The average date of the close of navigation
on the St. John River at Fredericton at the head of the
estuary in the last 126 years is November 26, and the Black
Ducks have left the inland waters in southern New Brunswick
by the first week in December as the freezing of the edges has
denied them access to the marsh vegetation. Thus the breeding population of eastern Canada is concentrated on its winter
range along the Atlantic seaboard from southern Newfoundland, Nova Scotia, and the Bay of Fundy shore of New Brunswick southward by early December. As they will be starting
north again by the third week in March, they spend just over
three months in winter quarters on the coast. The remaining
nine months of the year are spent in migrating to and from
the breeding grounds, and in raising the annual crop of young.
It is apparent that the greater part of the lives of this population of waterfowl is spent in Canada, and aside from regu-
lating the kill and improving winter range there is little
that can be done for them in the United States. This point
will be carried further in the section on management.

Flights of blacks originating in eastern Quebec have arrived in the Maritime Provinces by October 1st, since they
show up in the opening-day bags in New Brunswick. However, they do not seem to go farther south than eastern Maine
and southern Nova Scotia in this movement as they do not

appear in Massachusetts until early December. Toward the end of October these Quebec birds begin to leave the Bay of Fundy region, and apparently fly nonstop to Long Island and points south because they arrive in southern New Jersey at least three weeks before the first of them appear in Massachusetts. This movement continues throughout most of December.

The meager banding data available suggest that some of the birds from the Labrador coast seem to by-pass the Maritimes and fill the gap on the southern New England coast left by the Quebec birds during the middle of the shooting season. They arrive in the Carolinas and New Jersey at about the same time as the Quebec birds.

The Newfoundland blacks are late in moving south and do not arrive in Nova Scotia until early November. They are behind the birds from farther north in Quebec and Labrador, although some flights also by-pass southern New England and move into the Long Island-Maryland area about the same time as the remainder reach Nova Scotia.

The main St. Lawrence migration is as yet inadequately sampled to allow any definite statements regarding it, but the northern Lake Champlain stations show that some of this population has reached eastern New York by the middle of October, with the main flight following a month later. This flight apparently reaches southern New Jersey in one journey as very few birds are recovered in the intervening territory.

The Ontario flights bound for the South Atlantic states are from two to three weeks earlier than those from the northeast, and they reach the lower Mississippi and the Gulf Coast in the latter part of December. There is evidence both in this and in the northeast population that the far northern birds often pass on to the south of the local birds of southern Canada before the latter begin to move. This would appear to be a contradiction of the long-accepted theory that the "Northern Red-Legs," which appear in the late fall, are the last stragglers of big old adults from the far northern areas.

The duration of the fall migration from the time they leave Ungava Bay until the last flights of adults have reached the Bay of Fundy shore is about 80 days. This is the time that the migrants are in Canada. Some carry on south down the coast as far as the South Carolina-Georgia line, but it is not yet possible to say whether or not the Ungava Bay birds are the ones wintering on the northern extremity of the winter range, or whether they are scattered all down the coast. The birds from Labrador, the North Shore, and Newfoundland definitely show a wide dispersal on the winter range, so there is no reason to believe the far northern population would do differently, and the banding evidence previously mentioned shows that they often move south well before the local populations of more southern areas.

The air-line distance between the extremes of the principal summer and winter ranges, *i.e.,* from the south shore of

Ungava Bay to Cape Hatteras, is 14 degrees of latitude. Of these 14 degrees of latitude, or 1,440 miles, more than 900 are in Canadian territory, and the first 700 miles is a region where organized duck shooting is unknown. Therefore, the most important mortality factor of the flyway, the duck hunter, enters the picture only when the migration is within 200 miles of the United States border.

The Shooting Season

The Black Ducks moving up the St. Lawrence in the fall run into their first sport hunting on a serious scale at the eastern end of the Island of Orleans. Some shooting takes place all along the south shore of the river below the island, but it is nowhere as concentrated or as heavy as in the north channel of the island. Here the first clubs are found, and shooting is constant throughout the season. The famous club at Cap Tourmente makes an annual kill of Black Ducks and Greater Snow Geese which compares favorably with the shooting anywhere on the continent, and it is on the sandbanks and mudflats off this shore that the blacks make their first long stop on their journey upriver. They linger there until a hard freeze, coupled with a high tide and a strong east wind drives them over the towering Quebec Bridge and into the shelter of the Lake St. Peter marshes, or southward via Lake Champlain.

The method of hunting here always is from a blind over decoys, and many clubs have constructed artificial ponds on the marshes above highwater mark as there is a very strong tide to be considered. The feeding behavior of the ducks is typical of the fall and winter pattern followed all down the flyway. They raft in the channel during the day and fly into the marsh to feed only at dusk, returning to open water with the coming of daylight. For this reason most of the kill is made in the last half hour of shooting, or the first half hour in the morning. On Lake St. Peter many blinds are on off-shore islands, necessitating seaworthy boats to reach them, and the equipment needed there is quite elaborate.

In the Maritime Provinces, the great majority of the blacks are shot over decoys, but some are taken by stalking the wooded streams and beaver ponds of the bush country. The shooting of Black Ducks in this manner is almost as good a test of still-hunting ability as shooting a deer. They are exceedingly alert and wary, and the slightest sight or sound of the hunter reaching them will put them up.

The main shooting areas of New Brunswick are the North Shore, the Missiquash-Tantramar area on the Nova Scotia border, and the St. John estuary. Of these three major areas, the St. John estuary is by far the most important as over half of the total kill in the province is made there. Late season shooting takes place along the Bay of Fundy coast and in the Grand Manan Islands, but the kill does not approximate that of the St. John.

In Prince Edward Island the shooting is mostly on salt water habitats, but there are a few good inland areas, of which Pisguid Pond probably is the best. In Nova Scotia, duck shooting takes place all along the coast where suitable habitat is available, but the principal areas are along the New Brunswick border, on the east shore of Minas Basin, and on the wintering grounds at the extreme southern tip of the province in Yarmouth and Shelburne counties.

This latter area is the region where the famous tolling dogs have been developed. The dog is trained to play on the beach in sight of a raft of ducks. The curiosity of the ducks brings them in close to the shore to see what the dog is doing, and it deliberately leads them toward the blind and into range of the guns. No special breed of dog is used for this work, and many of them are of the farm collie type. This is a particularly deadly method of hunting waterfowl, and as both barrels usually are discharged into a closely packed flock on the water, it can scarcely be called sport. However, it provides waterfowl for the table of many a Nova Scotia home with a minimum of effort on the part of the hunter.

Shooting on the offshore ledges of the Bay of Fundy is sport of the most rugged type. The gunner is left on the ledge at low tide and is picked up by his tender at the last minute before the tide covers it. Since this type of shooting takes place usually in December, it is cold, raw sport of the hardest kind. However, large bags frequently are made by the hardy souls who go out on the ledges in rough weather, but few ducks are harder earned. The table qualities of the blacks shot there in December are considerably inferior to those of the St. John estuary, where they have been feeding on fresh-water vegetable foods. The foods of the coastal waters, being almost entirely marine, give the birds a fishy taste which is absent in those taken on fresh water.

This type of shooting is practiced in the Grand Manan Islands until late January, by which time the birds are paired and are getting ready to begin the spring migration. This late shooting is not sound conservation, as it breaks up the pairs, and the only thing that can be said for it is that the total kill probably is not large.

As they pass the United States border, the shooting becomes heavier as the gunners increase in numbers. Many are killed at Merrymeeting Bay in Maine and at other points along the coast. The next area of heavy killing is around Newburyport and Parker River in Massachusetts, and from there the birds move on to the gunners of Long Island Sound. Directly south of there they enter the most deadly killing ground of all, the region about Cape May, New Jersey. We have received a larger number of returns from our banded blacks from that region than from any other area. From there to Cape Hatteras the kill drops off, but a few stragglers have been reported from as far south as the Georgia line.

The returns of banded ducks shot during the open season show that the main breeding population of Black Ducks from eastern Canada winters along the coast from Newfoundand to Cape Hatteras, and the kill is distributed along this great length of seaboard. The areas mentioned above are the major killing grounds, as shown by the greater number of bands recovered there, but there also is a consistent distribution of recoveries along the coast between these areas.

This would seem to be at variance with Hagar (45), who says, when discussing the Cape Cod banding records: "The migration urge is spent by December 1; ducks arriving from the northeast after that date are very rarely recovered farther south . . . These findings . . . dispose of the possibility that southward migration (from Cape Cod) is a material consideration . . . ." Our records show quite clearly that our birds pass on well to the south of Cape Cod in numbers, and as the shooting season on the south coast of New Brunswick is just nearing its peak by December 1, it seems extremely doubtful whether all the birds between there and Cape Cod have stopped their southward movement and are in winter quarters. The number of birds present at that time on the New Brunswick coast is considerably greater than the wintering population so that there still is a southward migration taking place. Of 93 recoveries of Black Ducks banded at our stations in the northern breeding grounds and recovered south of Cape Cod, 56, or 60 per cent, were recovered after December 1. There is no way of knowing, however, if these birds had passed the Cape by that date as Hagar asserts, but this seems doubtful in the light of the date of departure of the late migrants from the Bay of Fundy area.

It will be seen, therefore, that the following states and provinces have a share in harvesting the annual crop of Black Ducks raised in eastern Canada:

1. Newfoundland	10. Connecticut
2. Quebec	11. New York
3. New Brunswick	12. New Jersey
4. Prince Edward Island	13. Delaware
5. Nova Scotia	14. Maryland
6. Maine	15. Virginia
7. New Hampshire	16. North Carolina
8. Massachusetts	17. South Carolina
9. Rhode Island	

These 5 provinces and 12 states are the areas where the kill must be adjusted to meet the harvestable surplus if the eastern flyway is not to be overshot. As practically all of the returns south of the United States border are coastal, it is only the shooting in the counties facing on the seashore that affects these birds. The inland shooting is provided by birds coming from more westerly breeding grounds in Ontario and the North Central States, and those areas also provide most of the blacks shot on the Atlantic coast south of Cape Hatteras, and almost all of those shot in the Mississippi Flyway.

Along this great stretch of coastline, and up the tidal mouths of the rivers, the hunter scans the sky the evening before and prays that a high tide and an east wind will bring the birds in to his decoys in the gray dawn as he crouches in his blind in the salt marsh. It is this combination of circumstances that gives him his best chance, for then the birds must use the upper edge of the marsh because of the tide, and because of the strong on-shore wind they cannot stay out in the rough water until after dark. When these conditions are fulfilled the hunter crouches lower in his blind and checks his gear carefully, because he knows that it may well be now or never for a limit on blacks this year.

If you are shooting in the estuary of the St. John in New Brunswick, what success might you expect? What will be the composition of your bag? Will you need a dog? Will you get young birds mostly, or will there be some big adults?

The success ratio for opening day on the St. John is given for four years in Table III, but this drops off after the opening flurry to a low in mid-season and revives as the last flights of adults come in from the North Shore at the end of the season.

You can expect, therefore, to shoot 4 ducks if you are out on Opening Day. You might get your limit of 7, but the chances are against it in most years. What species of ducks will they be? Table IV shows the species composition of the bag both on Opening Day and for the entire 1950 season.

Your bag probably will consist of 40 per cent blacks on the two opening days, but this will drop to 32 per cent if you keep shooting all season. The large number of unidenti-

TABLE III. SUCCESS RATIO OPENING 2 DAYS, ST. JOHN RIVER

Year	Gun/days	Total Ducks	Success Ratio ducks/gun day
1947	47.5	233	4.9
1948	37.5	161	4.3
1949	202.5	715	3.5
1950	54.5	270	4.9
Totals	342.0	1,379	
Average			4.0

fied ducks in this table is caused by the practice of some
hunters of plucking, cleaning and removing the head, legs
and wings in the field. If this has been done before a party
is reached by the checkers, they cannot identify the ducks,
which therefore can be included in only the success ratio
computation.

TABLE IV. SPECIES COMPOSITION—1950

Species	Opening 2 Days No.	%	All Season No.	%
Blacks	108	40.0	112	32.2
Ringnecks	44	16.3	58	16.6
Wood Ducks	30	11.1	32	9.2
Scaup	17	6.3	19	5.5
B. W. Teal	13	4.8	14	4.0
G. W. Teal	7	2.6	10	2.9
Goldeneye	1	0.4	53	15.2
Mallard	1	0.4	1	0.3
Unidentified	49	18.1	49	14.1
Totals	270	100.0	348	100.0

Will your birds be young or old? Male or female? Table V shows the sex and age ratios of five seasons bag in the estuary.

TABLE V.   SEX AND AGE RATIOS, ALL SPECIES,
ST. JOHN RIVER

Year	Total Ducks	Age Ratio Ad: Imm	Sex Ratio Male: Female
*1946	260	36:54	56:44
1947	181	24:76	50:50
1948	279	20:80	51:49
1949	304	41:59	53:47
1950	348	47:53	56:44
Total:	1,372		

* Opening day was September 15, 1946. All other years it was October 1st.

Over the whole season you may expect to get a few more young than adults and a few more males than females. You will shoot mostly young birds during the opening flurry, but this will be offset by a preponderance of adults in the late-season bag.

How many ducks will you lose, and will you require a dog? Parties hunting with dogs in the estuary lose about 16 per cent of their total bag, and parties without dogs lose about 24 per cent; so the use of a trained retriever definitely increases the "take home pay" of the hunter, as well as being a sound conservation practice. The tall grasses and sedges of this country make hunting cripples without a dog almost hopeless.

The answers given here to the questions every duck hunter asks apply to only one small district of the region where the ducks are harvested, but it is a section at the beginning of the line. From there south the coastal flight of Black Ducks is diluted more and more by additions of other species from more westerly breeding grounds, and these figures will not apply.

Chapter VI

The Distribution of the Black Duck

THE WINTER RANGE

WHEN THE blacks are concentrated on their winter range by the end of December, they occupy the smallest area in their annual cycle. The winter range starts at the mouth of the Rio Grande on the Texas coast and extends northeastward to just south of the southern tip of Lake Michigan, from there eastward along the southern shores of Lakes Erie and Ontario and across the mountains to the New England coast. The coastal range runs north into extreme southwestern New Brunswick, the southern tip of Nova Scotia, and the south coast of Newfoundland.

All of the country southeast of this line is winter range except the southern tip of Florida. The northeastern population occupies the coastal strip from Cape Hatteras north to Newfoundland, and the Great Lakes-James Bay birds occupy the remainder of the range. There is considerable overlap of these two populations, and drakes, particularly, may mate with a female from the other region and follow her to her home breeding grounds the following spring, but usually the two populations remain distinct.

Some of the outstanding areas of winter range that should receive mention here are Merrymeeting Bay in Maine, Cape Cod, Long Island Sound, and the 30-mile-long Great South Bay on the south shore of Long Island. Merrymeeting Bay is formed by the mouths of six rivers coming together to form an irregular shallow bay 18 miles long and up to 3 miles wide. The bay freezes over in winter, but two-thirds of the flats are exposed at low tide and so provide a feeding ground for the waterfowl. The area is a prolific producer of duck foods with wildrice and bulrushes predominating. Many kinds of pondweeds also can be found in the innumerable small channels. Ducks from both the St. Lawrence and the coast use this area extensively. In this region, when you say "duck" you mean a Black Duck, as it provides the bulk of the shooting. This area is shot heavily, and many banded ducks are recovered there.

The great hook of Cape Cod stretching out into the Atlantic makes a natural stopping place for the migrating blacks. For many years extensive baiting was carried out there in connection with banding operations, and this may have helped hold birds that otherwise would have gone farther south. The salt marshes are extensive and always have been the winter home of numbers of blacks.

The Connecticut shore of Long Island Sound is one of the first places mentioned as a wildfowling area on this continent. Fluctuations in the food supply govern the numbers of wintering ducks, and with the last disappearance of the eelgrass the brant and geese passed on to the south. Pollution is a major problem there because of the proximity of large industrial centers, and it has affected the food supply. There are many ponds in the eastern end of Long Island which are used by blacks, particularly during heavy blows, and there again "a high tide and an east wind" applies.

Great South Bay along the south coast of Long Island is 30 miles long and about 4 miles wide, and is separated from

Photo by A. D. Benson

Plate XXVI. The most important assembly point in Newfoundland is this marsh at the mouth of the Grand Codroy River in the southwest corner of the island.

Photo by W. H. Carrick

Plate XXVII. The large old adults are the last to arrive in the fall and they were long thought to be a different species because of their greater size and full winter plumage.

Plate XXVIII. In late fall the blacks raft during the day in exposed locations where they cannot be approached unseen. The lee of this gravel bar in Grand Lake, New Brunswick, is used for this purpose.

Photo by W. B. Catrick

Plate XXIX. Single left! Coming right In!

Plate XXX. The feeding grounds during winter and on spring migration. Between tides on the Bay of Fundy coast.

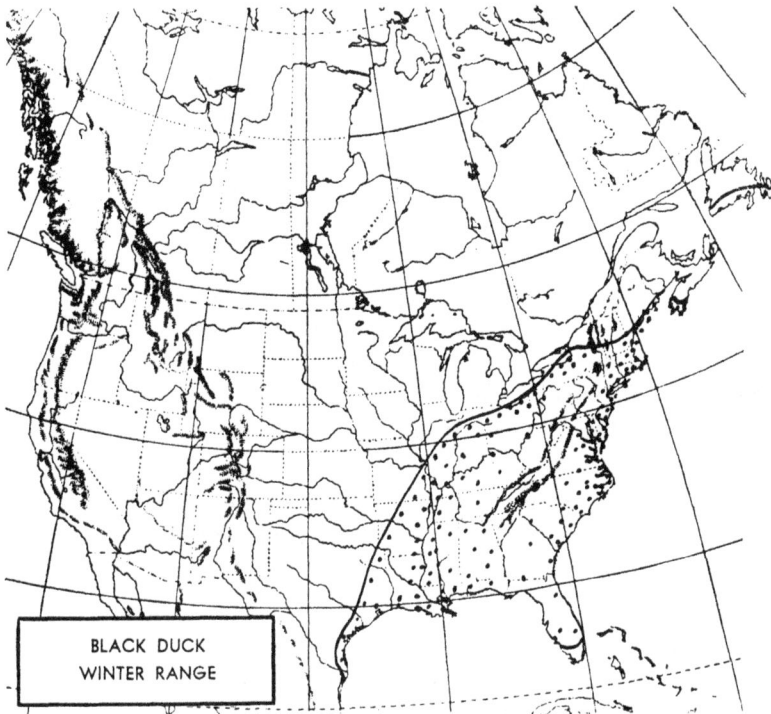

BLACK DUCK
WINTER RANGE

the open ocean by a narrow strip of sand dunes. This area was hit heavily by the eelgrass blight but is showing good recovery at this writing. It has been a famous shooting ground for a long time, and blacks make up the bulk of the bag.

The Barnegat Bay region is a 100-mile stretch of small bays, rivers and marshes between Bay Head and Cape May on the Jersey coast, and a very heavy annual kill is made there. Moving southward along the coast as the ducks do, we come to the Chesapeake Bay country. This great bay with its tributaries is said to have between four and five thousand miles of shoreline and is almost 200 miles long. The combined lengths of the navigable waters of the bay and its tributaries are over 1,750 miles, and beyond the navigable waters lie thousands of acres of marshes, sloughs, guts, ponds and leads, all rich in wildrice and pondweeds.

The Eastern Shore of Virginia is another favorite wintering

area for many Black Ducks, Canvasback, Redhead, and scaup, as well as geese, brant and swan. This area was hit heavily by the eelgrass blight, and with the eelgrass went the ducks; but as this plant re-establishes itself, the ducks will return to their old grounds. The James and Potomac rivers also offer first-class winter range in this same region, and to the south the great brackish bays in Princess Anne County, Virginia, are used heavily. In this region, Back Bay has been noted as a wildfowling center for more than a century.

Currituck Sound to the south and the hundred-mile-long Pamlico Sound are the most important wintering grounds of brant and Canada Geese on the whole coast. There the shooting is done from stake-blinds which dot the tide flats as far as five miles from the nearest land, but this type of shooting is not very effective for blacks, since they prefer the salt marshes to the open sand reefs and resort to the latter only after a spell of freezing weather has closed the marshes. The most important duck here is the Pintail, which makes up the greater part of the bag.

Many blacks from the Great Lakes winter on the South Carolina coast, but this is too far south for any but stragglers from the northeast. Western blacks also winter in moderate numbers in northern Florida, where the Indian River, Mosquito Lagoon, Banana River, and the Ten Thousand Islands opposite Cocoa are the principal areas used. The nights are spent in the mangrove-fringed pools and the days on the larger bodies of open water. Most of the shooting is in the early morning and late evening, the same as it is all the way up the flyway to the Eskimo hunters of Ungava Bay.

Westward along the Gulf coast the blacks drop in importance as game ducks as they are swallowed up in the millions of Mallards, Pintail, Baldpate, and Teal of the Mississippi and Central flyways.

THE BREEDING RANGE

The northern limit of the breeding range in the east is the limit of trees in Ungava. The mountains of the northern Labrador coast exclude this region, and I have drawn the eastern limit as the western slopes of these mountains. The Mealy Mountains south of Lake Melville are not breeding habitat and have been excluded. Over the rest of this vast region the blacks breed in widely scattered pairs.

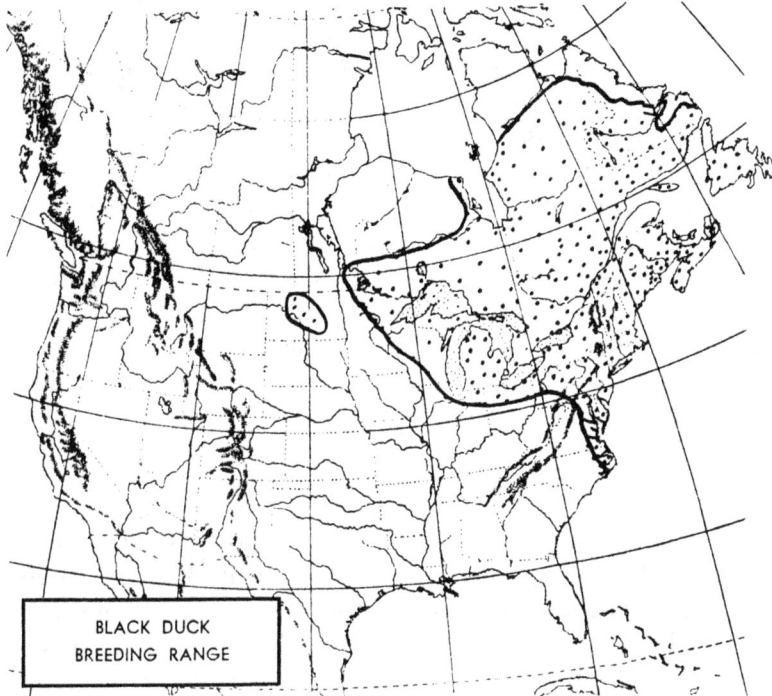

BLACK DUCK
BREEDING RANGE

The Leaf River drainage is the northern limit of trees across the base of the Ungava Peninsula, and the line runs out to the coast of Hudson Bay at Richmond Gulf. The three specimens collected at Cape Dorset, Baffin Island, in June were heads only, taken from an Eskimo's cooking pot; so it is not possible to say whether or not they were a pair and an extra drake, and they cannot be used as a breeding record.

Blacks breed in the ponds above tidewater on both sides of James Bay, and across the interior of Ontario south of the Albany River to the extreme southeast corner of Manitoba. An isolated breeding area for a few pairs is reported in North Dakota (47), but the main range is east of a line running from southeastern Manitoba to the southern end of Lake Michigan. From there the boundary runs due east to the coastal regions, and south to Cape Hatteras.

Breeding records are lacking from the west shore of Hudson Bay, but Austin (7) says, the Black Duck "breeds from the west side of Hudson Bay to Cape Chidley . . ." The Cape Chidley region is a most unsuitable breeding area, since it is mostly bare rock, and Mr. Bob May of George River reports (*Ibid.*) that in many years' fieldwork in this region he never has seen young Black Ducks, and he is of the opinion that they do not breed north of the trees.

This, then, is the breeding range, the humid region of northeastern North America, and it is occupied by the females and young from March to early July. The males wander outside the northern and western boundaries of this range to moult as soon as they leave the females in June; so they are the first to arrive on the post-breeding range.

The Post-Breeding Range

Adults and flying young have been reported in small numbers in all three prairie provinces and in the Northwest Territories, and a specimen was collected in California (42). The farthest north is on the Thelon River (25) and Chesterfield Inlet (110), and the farthest northwest is in the Athabaska Delta, where a specimen was secured for the National Museum of Canada by Ducks Unlimited.

In the northeast, they move out to tidewater all around the coastline of Quebec and Labrador, and on the Ontario shore of Hudson Bay and James Bay. This movement often is due north and is made with no regard to the points of the compass. The birds of the Labrador taiga move north to the salt meadows of False River and the tide flats of Ungava Bay, and those of northern Ontario fly out to James Bay. Along the St. Lawrence the backwoods lakes are abandoned in favor of the tidal marshes, and in the Maritimes and Newfoundland they concentrate in the river mouths and bays.

At this time they are occupying a larger area than at any

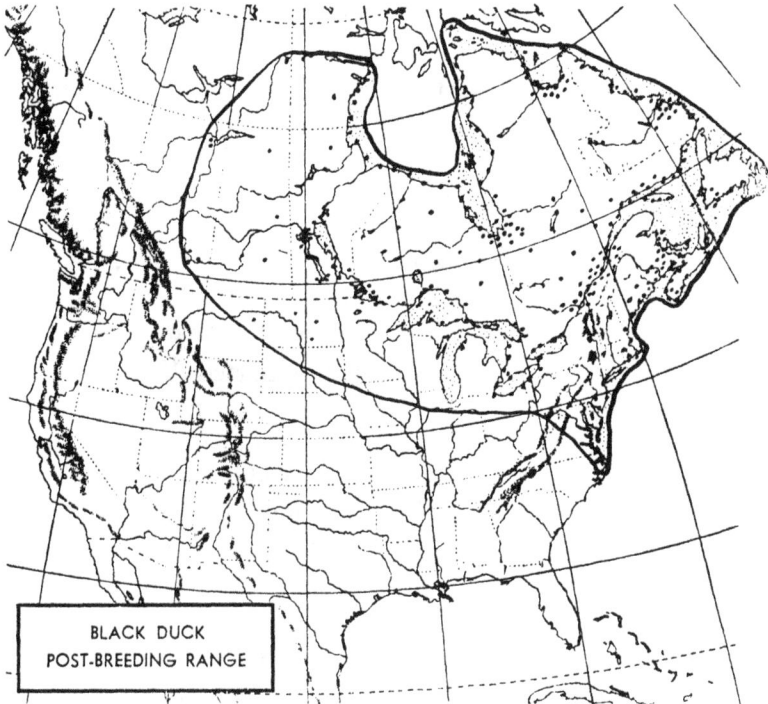

BLACK DUCK
POST-BREEDING RANGE

other time of the year and may be found from Cape Hatteras in the south to Baffin Island in the north, and from Newfoundland in the east to Alberta in the west. They will occupy this expanded range until the first frosts in the fall start to roll back the northern edge.

There is evidence that the boundary of this western post-breeding range has fluctuated greatly in the last hundred years. The bones of this species were found at the site of the ancient Indian village of Aztalan near Madison, Wisconsin (8), and this is of particular interest as in several subsequent records of waterfowl taken in this region the Black Duck is not mentioned. A list of ducks taken at Faville Grove, Wisconsin, about 1883 does not include blacks, and the Chase *Journal* shows no blacks taken by the author in the environment of Lake Wingra, Wisconsin, between 1873-1896. During this latter period the author of the *Journal* shot 1,500 other

ducks of 17 species; so his record is good evidence of their
absence at that time.

The first specimen taken at East Shoal Lake in Manitoba
was shot in 1896, and by 1910 blacks frequently were seen
in the late summer in that area, and to take one or two in a
day on the marsh there was not uncommon. From 1910 to
1925 there was a steady increase, and in September 1923 a
hunter shot 12 on opening day with a single-barrel shotgun.
In 1937, another hunter shot 9 out of a total of 21 during
a flight of Mallards, and 6 of these were immature birds.

As long ago as 1890, McFarlane reported blacks on the
Anderson River, where he listed them as not uncommon.
The nearest record to this is Clarke's (*Ibid.*) from the Thelon
River, and no confirmation of the Anderson River record
has been made since. Preble (101) was informed by A. F.
Camsell of Fort Simpson that they sometimes were shot
at that post in the spring, but since then there have been no
records from that region.

Phillips (94) states: "Seton (Auk, 1908, pp 450) gives three
records from Shoal Lake and one for Lake Manitoba, and
says it abounds on the Athabasca River. I do not know upon
what this last statement is based. Neither am I able to ex-
plain McFarlane's (1908) statement that hundreds are seen
at Cumberland House and Fort Chipewyan, and the species
is not uncommon on the Anderson River. On a recent trip
to the Athabasca region, where he spent the whole breeding
season, Mr. F. Harper got no information of Black Ducks
having been seen there. However, Preble (1908), another
Biological Survey collector, was told that it occurred occasionally at Fort Simpson, on the Upper MacKenzie River."
However blacks were seen in the Athabaska delta by Ducks
Unlimited fieldmen in 1940, and, as previously mentioned, a
specimen was collected and placed in the National Museum to
establish this record.

As long ago as 1822 Macoun says, "I have never noticed
the Black Duck in any part of the North-West, nor do I know
that others have." It would appear therefore that at the

time it was being reported in the far northwest it was absent from the southwestern edge of the post-breeding range in Wisconsin. Later when the northwestern records could not be confirmed (about 1920), it was returning to Wisconsin so that there is evidence of drastic fluctuations in the boundaries of the northwestern and western edges of this range. There are not sufficient data on hand to formulate any conclusions as to the cause and extent of these fluctuations, but they are a recognized phenomenon in other species of birds and particularly in the songbird group.

Additional evidence of this ebb and flow of the Black Duck population on the western edge of its range is shown in the U. S. Fish & Wildlife Service's data from the Seney National Wildlife Refuge, Schoolcraft, Michigan. The peak concentration and the estimated total young produced in the ten years prior to 1953 are shown below.

Year (May-August)	Peak Concentration	Est. Total Young
1944	8,500	200
1945	6,500	500
1946	6,000	400
1947	150	800
1948	500	800
1949	400	400
1950	1,800	600
1951	900	350
1952	2,000	1,500
1953	2,200	1,200

In this ten-year period the number of birds using the refuge decreased drastically, but at the same time the nesting population made an even more drastic increase. How much of this increase in breeders is attributable to management practices conducted at the refuge and how much to natural ebb and flow, of course, is not known.

At the Mud Lake and Rice Lake National Wildlife Refuges

in Minnesota the annual production varied from 0 to 1,400 blacks on the former, and from 0 to 260 blacks on the latter in the period from 1942 through 1953. The spring and fall peak concentrations also varied greatly here and at the Waubay Refuge in South Dakota.

It is apparent that this state of flux in the western boundaries of the range still is continuing, and apparently has been going on for at least one hundred years.

Chapter VII

Black Duck Management in Eastern Canada

POPULATION MEASUREMENTS

THE FIRST step in any management program must be to develop methods of measuring the various properties of the population it is desired to manage. There are five principal periods in which waterfowl populations can be measured on the breeding grounds, but only the first four are of any value in estimating the fall flight. They are spring flight, the territorial period, brood counts, the late summer concentration period, and finally, the fall flight.

The method used to measure the composition of Black Duck flights during spring migration was discussed in the chapter on that period. The method showed the composition of the flight and the times when the unpaired birds passed through, but no method of correlating these spring measurements with actual populations on the marshes in the fall has come to light. The number of variables between the arrival of the breeding stock and the harvesting of the annual crop is so great that no satisfactory method of forecasting fall flights from spring inventories has been developed.

Counts of territorial males and pairs have yielded good results in the west where the nesting cover and territories both are accessible and are close to each other. In the east, however, and particularly with the Black Duck, the territories usually are inaccessible and scattered widely, and the drake frequently moves from one territory to another as he is forced off his first choice by differences in water level. This makes a count of territorial drakes much more difficult to make and of doubtful accuracy in most regions in the northeast.

Brood counts yield valuable data on the nesting chronology and the productive capacity of the species and are carried out from the day the first broods appear to the date the last young are awing. They do not in themselves, however, yield data on actual populations, so that an estimate of the annual crop must await the period when the young are awing, have emerged from the heavy cover of the creeks and backwoods ponds, and are concentrated on the marshes. Then, and only then, can the annual production of waterfowl of any region of eastern Canada be seen.

For these reasons the only reliable indicator of the fall flight that we have been able to develop is a census of selected study areas after most of the young are awing but before the southward drift becomes too apparent. The period selected for this count in southern New Brunswick is July 16 to August 17. By that date, the great majority of the young are awing in most years, and the only species which has begun the southward movement is the Blue-winged Teal. The southward movement of this species is just becoming noticeable by the end of the census on the Grand Lake marshes of New Brunswick.

The two major flights of Black Ducks in the area are the coastal flight coming south through the Maritime Provinces and along the Maine coast, and the St. Lawrence flight coming southwest up the St. Lawrence and overland to the Atlantic coast. No permanent study area has been established in the St. Lawrence migration route at this writing, but in 1945 the first inventory was taken of a 32,500-acre study area in the estuary of the St. John River in New Brunswick. The estuary contains at least 38,000 acres of waterfowl habitat and has as high a population of local breeding ducks as any similar area in the northeast.

It is stated by Raymond (104) that the St. John is the largest river on the Atlantic seaboard with the exception of the St. Lawrence, and its estuary from the Reversing Falls at Saint John to the head of tidewater above Fredericton is more than 90 miles long. It is in this estuary that the great spring and fall flights gather, and where the local breeders nest and bring off their broods. Above this, there are more than 400 miles of river, once navigable by river steamboat, but most of the channels have filled in now, and 2,630 miles of rivers and tributary streams navigable by boats and canoes (104).

As would be expected of a river of this size in this latitude, there are strong spring freshets. An indication of the strength of these freshets may be gained from the record of a canoe journey from Grand Falls to Fredericton, a distance of 133 miles, made at the height of the freshet in 14 hours and 46 minutes by two men who made "a short stop" at Woodstock on the way (104).

The study area is located on the east bank of the estuary in the area known as the Maugerville-Sheffield Intervale. It consists of the Grand Lake marshes, the marshes and low-lands between the main river and Maquapit and French Lakes, the watershed of Portobello Creek back to the 25-foot contour, and the coves and marshes at its mouth. The whole area is located at the junction of the Grand Lake drainage with that of the main St. John. The tributaries entering here drain an area of 1,470 square miles and are surpassed by the drainage of only the Aroostook and the Tobique.

At this junction point an area of about 50 square miles

is submerged to a depth of 10 feet by the spring freshet. The water rises rapidly, and there is an annual loss by drowning among the moose and deer of the lowlands. The whole of the lower St. John is a "drowned river" in the geological sense, and the southern coast of New Brunswick still is sinking. The study area itself is part of a region which was at one time a lake about 35 miles in length and the same in breadth. Today, Grand Lake and the others of the chain are all that remain of the larger lake. The marshes have been formed by the deposition of sediment from the annual freshet upon the clay of the original lake bed, and the process still is going on. The whole southwest end of the remaining lakes are filling in, and the submerged aquatics are established now as far as half a mile from shore. The marshes are extending into the lakes and the landward side is solidifying and becoming wild hay meadows. The underlying geological formation is Pennsylvanian sandstones, shales, and conglomerates of the Carboniferous period.

This study area was chosen because it is accessible from the outside, and is large enough to give true wilderness conditions in the interior. Six species of ducks nest there, and the normal bird population of the northeast uses the marshes and flooded lowlands in the summer months. The big game of the region, moose and deer, use it intensively as summer range, and the common marsh furbearers—muskrat, beaver, mink, and otter—also are present. Raccoons are quite common and do some damage to tree-nesting ducks. Foxes are numerous at this writing. The ecology of the fresh-water habitats of southeastern Canada is fairly represented in this area, and the annual population changes can be considered as typical of conditions throughout the region in general as any one marsh can be.

The annual inventory of breeding ducks was made in the following manner. The study area was broken down into four types of waterfowl habitat bounded by two types of shoreline. These habitat types were (1) open water, (2) open marsh, (3) cultivation, (4) hardwood swamp; and each type

was bounded by shoreline classified either as Perimeter shore-line or Slough shoreline. The areas of the four types of habitat and the lengths of the two types of shoreline then were measured from an inch-to-the-mile map.

The area was found to consist of 49 per cent hardwood swamp, 30 per cent open marsh, 14 per cent cultivation, and 7 per cent open water. There were 73.4 miles of perimeter shoreline and 108.5 miles of slough shoreline. The dominant species of the hardwood swamp type were: Red Maple, *Acer rubrum;* Silver Maple, *Acer saccharinum;* Black Ash, *Fraxinus nigra;* and American Elm, *Ulmus americana.*

The open marsh type consisted of large areas of cordgrass, *Spartina pectinata,* and bluejoint, *Calamagrostis,* surrounded by a fringe of Three-square and River Bulrush, Spikerush, Pickerelweed, and Wildrice. The submerged aquatics of importance to waterfowl are at least six species of pondweeds— wild celery, smartweed, coontail, bladderwort, burreed, and duckweed—and there are approximately six tons per acres of vegetable and animal food available for dabbling ducks in the top two inches of the sloughs at the peak of the growing season.

The waterfowl count was made from a canoe by cruising the shoreline in good weather between July 16 and August 17 each year from 1945-1950. The waterfowl were recorded by species, age, sex, and by the type of shoreline they were inhabiting. This count covered as much as 98 per cent of the shoreline of the study area in several years. Every effort was made to avoid duplication, and when it was obvious that the ducks were being driven up a creek ahead of the canoe, the count was discontinued and taken up again above that point a day or more later. The stealthy approach of the canoe usually caused the non-flying broods to gather around the female at the edge of the grass to stare at it before they skittered away a short distance and hid in the vegetation. This behavior gave an excellent opportunity to count them, and the broods that hid before they could be counted fully usually could be found again an hour later, not far from the same place, and recounted.

The cruise tally was recorded by species in ducks per mile of shoreline for both types of shoreline. The sample then was applied to the whole to give an approximation of the total population. Many moulting females undoubtedly were missed in this count, since they stay in heavy cover and have to be driven into the open, but the trend rather than the total population is the object of the count, and this is shown clearly.

The total population and the number of ducks per square mile of open marsh on this area between 1945 and 1950 is shown in Table VI.

TABLE VI. WATERFOWL POPULATION AND DENSITY, NEW BRUNSWICK STUDY AREA, 1945-1950

Year	Total Population	Ducks/Square Mile of Open Marsh
1945	1,689	111.9
1946	808	53.5
1947	973	69.4
1948	1,270	84.1
1949	2,495	165.2
1950	2,380	157.6

The drastic decline in breeding ducks in this area in 1946-1947 is shown clearly in these data. The species composition of the population on the area in 1950 is shown in Table VII.

All breeding species have shown fluctuations in the period of this study, but the Black Duck has remained the dominant breeder throughout; hence this year may be taken an indicative of conditions approaching normal on the marsh. Black Ducks, Wood Ducks and ringnecks make up over 80 per cent of the breeding population each year, and Fig. III shows the trends of these species in the period of study.

Both the Black Duck and the ringneck are heavily shot game ducks, but the Wood Duck is a protected species. It is interesting to note that the fluctuations in numbers of the Wood Duck roughly parallel those of the other two species, indicating that the causes of these fluctuations may be other than hunting pressure. On the other hand, the smaller numbers of Wood Duck may be affected as much by the small illegal gun pressure they receive as the more numerous blacks are by the heavy legal pressure.

TABLE VII. SPECIES COMPOSITION, NEW BRUNSWICK STUDY AREA, 1950

Species	% of Total
Black Duck	54.7
Wood Duck	14.5
Ringneck	12.5
Blue-winged Teal	9.1
Green-winged Teal	6.4
Goldeneye	2.1
Mallard	0.3
Unidentified	0.3
Scaup	0.1
Total	100.0

THE SHAPE OF THE POPULATION CURVE

The literature yields some clues to the abundance of Black Ducks in the early days of settlement of the northeast. Raymond (*Ibid.*) quoting the early settlers of the St. John says: "Wild game was vastly more abundant in this country when it was discovered by Europeans than it is today . . . Wildfowl ranged the coasts and marshes and frequented the rivers in incredible numbers. Baird says that at certain seasons they were so abundant on the islands (in the St. John) that by the skillful use of a club right and left they could bring down birds as big as ducks with every blow. Denys speaks of immense flocks of wild pigeons." The same author quotes Dr. Hannay that in 1638 "wildfowl of all kinds abounded along the marsh and interval lands of the St. John."

In 1717, Samuel Penhallow, the historian, describes a duck hunt he witnessed on the Kennebec River in Maine in which the Indians killed 4,600 ducks without the use of guns. Our study area was described by Beamsley Glazier in 1764 as

Plate **XXXI.** Baiting up for the night's activities. Baie Johan Beetz, P.Q.

Plate **XXXII.** A night's catch on the North Shore of the Gulf of St. Lawrence. Blacks in a trap at Baie Johan Beetz, P.Q.

Photo by D. A. Benson

Plate XXXIII. The Great Horned Owl, a most destructive trap robber. Taken in a duck trap where it had killed all captive ducks in its characteristic manner by decapitation.

Photo by C. O. Bartlett

Plate XXXIV. A dangerous trap robber which must be destroyed discreetly as it is money in the pocket to the local trappers. A mink caught raiding a duck trap on the North Shore of the Gulf of St. Lawrence.

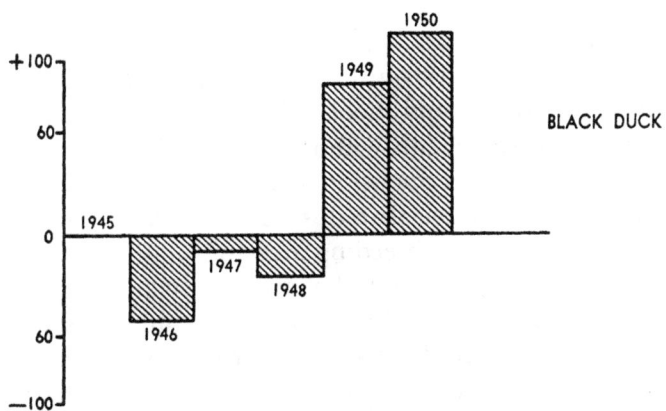

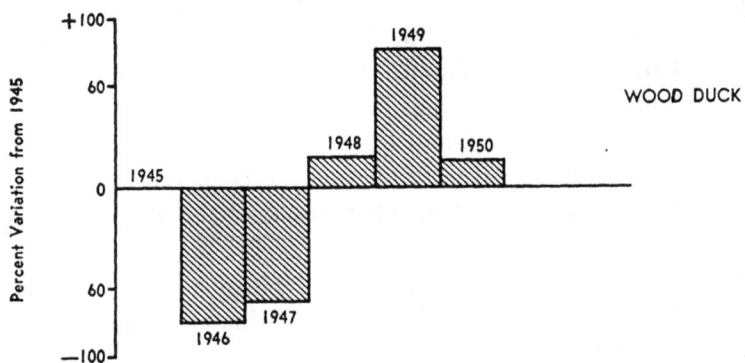

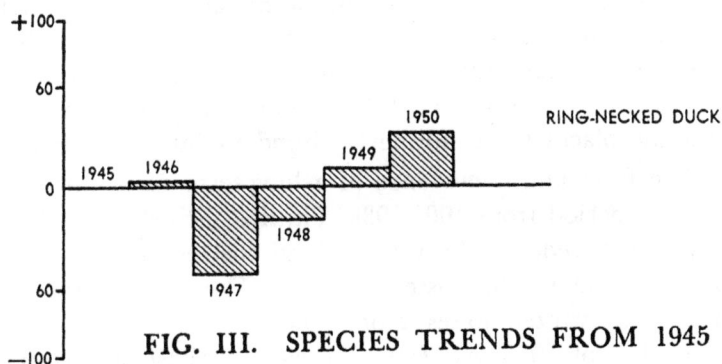

FIG. III. SPECIES TRENDS FROM 1945

follows: "Wildfowl of all kinds, cocks, snipes, and partridges are so plentiful that the gentleman who was with me swore it was no sport, as he could shoot three or four at a shot."

Compare these statements with those of Phillips and Lincoln (95) who state: "An impression exists among some people, even some ornithologists, that this northeast region was once far more important as a breeding area for wildfowl than it is now. There is little reason to believe any such thing. Wood ducks have become scarce through constant summer shooting, and hole-nesting species have suffered through scarcity of nesting sites, but there is no reason to believe that there has been any marked change in the breeding distribution of the more important game species."

It is interesting to contrast this last statement with the records of Fort Latour (Saint John) and Port Royal (Annapolis Royal in Nova Scotia), where the garrisons were fed on the thousands of goose eggs gathered around the forts, and some of the eggs were hatched and the goslings sent to the King of France as an example of the bounty of the new land. Canada Geese are not known to nest south of the St. Lawrence today.

The Black Duck is not mentioned specifically in these early reports, but as it always has been the dominant species of this flyway, we may assume it to have been present in numbers to correspond to the general abundance. Forbush (*Ibid.*) quotes Wilson as saying that in 1811 there were "at least 10 Black Ducks for every goose or brant, and probably more," and the same author quotes Samuels as saying that in 1870 the Black Duck was "the most abundant of all our freshwater ducks." In 1887, however, the same author quotes from Clark that the blacks were "formerly abundant but now rare."

The foregoing is evidence of a long-term downward trend. For the period from 1900-1930, Phillips (96) shows a definite downward trend in the western-bred species but no evidence of a decline in the eastern species. The same author (97) discussing winter losses along the Atlantic seaboard says: "The fall of 1933 was followed by the disastrous winter of

1934-1935, plus the complete failure of the eelgrass crop; our local ducks have scarcely shown any recovery up to the date of this writing." The low point seems to have been reached during this period, and the reports of the Atlantic Flyway Biologist of the U. S. Fish and Wildlife Service indicate a steady increase from 1937 through 1939. The peak apparently was reached about 1940, and the population showed no major changes until the major decrease in 1946 noted at the beginning of this study.

As the "duck depression" of the 1930's generally is supposed to have been caused by the dry part of the drought cycle in the west, it is of interest to note that it also occurred in the northeast, where drought never is a severe limiting factor. The low of 1946 was noticed in the western-bred ducks before it became apparent in the east, and the records of clubs on the St. Lawrence show that the low of the 1930's reached the bottom about a year after it was passed on the prairies. This suggests that these depressions move across the country from west to east, as has been noted already in the violently cyclic species such as grouse and snowshoe hares. The short-term trend is shown in Fig. III and indicates that the bottom of the latest depression was passed in 1946-1947, and that there was a steady increase from 1948 through 1950.

The evidence, therefore, indicates that the population curve of the Black Duck showed a gradual but steady decline until about the end of the nineteenth century, when it stabilized near its present level. There is no evidence of drastic changes in the next 30 years, but the curve depressed sharply in the mid-1930's in common with the other waterfowl species of the continent. The recovery from this low to the succeeding high covered the next five years, and the high was maintained for another five years. By 1945, a decline was becoming noticeable again in the western part of the breeding range, and in 1946, a drastic decrease was obvious in the east. The low level was maintained through two breeding seasons and then definite signs of recovery were seen. In 1950, the breeding population on the study area still was rising.

There is not as yet sufficient evidence to justify definite statements on the shape of the population curve, as we have no detailed evidence prior to about 1930. The last two peak lows were approximately 10 years apart, but proof of cyclic behavior must await further data. The study area data show that the population fluctuates violently on individual marshes, and the tendency to generalize must be guarded against. However, it may be said that the curve is not flat, and that there is no evidence of cyclic behavior. Rather, the evidence indicates that the population fluctuates from year to year within fairly narrow limits, and that major depressions occur at unknown intervals.

Gause (38) showed that variations in numbers may be a purely biological characteristic of a species divorced completely from environmental factors, and there is some evidence that this observation may be true of certain species of waterfowl. The fact that large decreases were noted in the heavily shot game ducks in 1946 would at first glance seem to suggest that overshooting was responsible. However, the protected Wood Duck also showed an 80 per cent decrease in breeders the following year, which would seem to cast some doubt on the overshooting theory.

Fig. IV shows a comparison of the size of broods of blacks and ringnecks, when still in the down, between the years 1946 and 1950. These two species were the only ones for which sufficient data were available to plot this curve.

Black Ducks were at their peak low in 1946, and ringnecks in 1947. It will be noted that at this time both species showed a peak high in brood size, which tapered off as the species recovered. There was a late spring with flood losses in 1947, and this might have been expected to cause the average young broods to be smaller because of renesting. This, however, was not the case, and the broods averaged larger than in any other year of the study except the last for ringnecks. This suggests that the reason may be biological, the result of some change in the laying potential of the females in periods of adversity, rather than environmental due to some specially

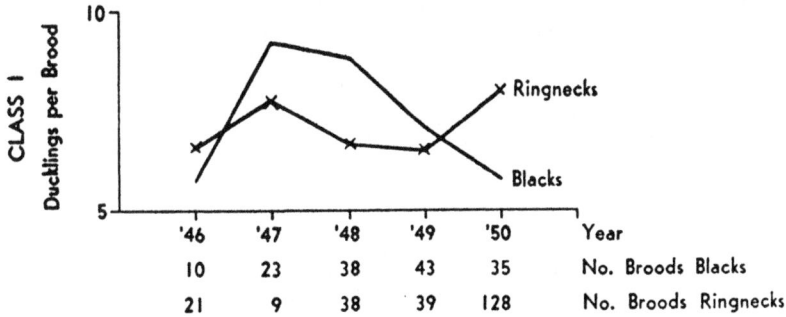

FIG. IV. BROOD SIZE COMPARISON, CLASS I BROODS
1946-1950

favorable external factor. The peak is not as distinct in ringnecks as in blacks, but Fig. III shows that ringnecks did not fluctuate nearly as violently as did the blacks in that period, and therefore the recovery potential was not called upon to the same degree.

The recovery potential of the Black Duck may be measured against the standards drawn up for Mallard and Redhead by Hochbaum (56). This comparison is shown in Table VIII.

The Mallard exhibits 13 characteristics advancing recovery and only 2 retarding it, but the reverse is true of the Redhead. The Black Duck is in the same position as the Mallard except that hunting pressure on the Black Duck is rather higher than on the Mallard because there are fewer and less acceptable buffer species in its range. The Black Duck may, therefore, be judged as a species with high recovery potential from periods of adversity, and this ability to come back is illustrated in Fig. IV.

A Life Equation for Black Ducks

At this point in the study it is possible to attempt a life equation computation based on the factors for which actual measurements have been made, and assuming values for the others, to bring the population back to the starting point.

TABLE VIII. COMPARISON OF RECOVERY POTENTIAL IN MALLARD, REDHEAD AND BLACK DUCK

(Mallard and Redhead data from Hochbaum 1946)

Condition	Mallard	Adv	Ret	Redhead	Adv	Ret	Black	Adv	Ret
Numbers	Relatively high	x	–	Relatively low	–	x	Relatively high	x	–
Breeding Range									
A—Regional	Extensive	x	–	Limited	–	x	Extensive	x	–
B—Local	Spread	x	–	Concentrated	–	x	Spread	x	–
Pioneering	Rapid	x	–	Slow	–	x	Rapid	x	–
Sex Properties	More evenly balanced sex ratios helps Mallards and blacks.								
Nesting									
A—Time	Early nesting hazardous	–	x	Middle nesting less hazardous	x	–	Early nesting hazardous	–	x
B—Place	Land nests vulnerable to more hazards	–	x	Water nests vulnerable to fewer hazards	x	–	Land and tree nests vulnerable	–	x
C—Waste	Little	x	–	Great	–	x	Little	x	–
D—Response to management.	Rapid	x	–	Slow	–	x	Rapid	x	–
Rearing									
A—Hatching date	Early	x	–	Late	–	x	Early	x	–
B—Growth rate	Rapid	x	–	Slow	–	x	Fairly rapid	x	–
C—Period with hen	Full brood period	x	–	Abandoned before full-grown	–	x	Full brood period	x	–
Hunting									
A—Condition	Young in good condition when season opens	x	–	Young poorly conditioned when season opens	–	x	Young in good condition	x	–
B—Hunting pressure	Relatively light in proportion to numbers	x	–	Relatively heavy in proportion to numbers	–	x	Relatively heavy	–	x
C—Wariness	One of the most wary game birds	x	–	One of the least wary game birds	–	x	Very wary	x	–
		13	2		2	13		12	3

By this method, some approximation of the unknown losses may be arrived at, which can be refined as data accumulate.

Assuming a flock of 100 Black Ducks leaves the Grand Lake marshes in New Brunswick in the fall, and at the same time next year there again is a flock of 100 ready to start south, or in other words a population which has remained stable throughout one year, then the gain and loss statement of this population must be close to the following:

LIFE EQUATION FOR A STABLE POPULATION OF BLACK DUCKS. I

Date	Item and Computation	Gain	Loss	Current Pop.
Oct. 1	Population made up of 12 broods @ 6.3 ...... 76 24 adults .... 24 —— 100			100
Jan. 1 Mar. 1 Apr. 18	Hunting Loss Crippling Loss (21% Hunting Loss) Winter Loss 20 prs. nest. Nesting Success 60% incl. renests. 12 Successful nests @ 9 eggs....108 12 prs. adults .... 24 16 unpaired adults .... 16 —— 148	108	60	148
May 30	Egg Loss 11% 12 broods hatched @ 8 ..96 ducklings 12 prs. adults ....24 16 unpaired adults ....16 —— 136		12	136
Oct. 1	Juvenile Mortality 21% ducklings hatched. Adult Mortality. 12 broods @ 6.3.......76 24 adults ....24 —— 100		20 16	100
		108	108	

The average-sized brood reaching flying age is 6.3; so the sample population of 100 ducks is composed of 12 broods and 24 adults, which may or may not have been their parents. Hunting loss, crippling loss, and winter loss are unknowns at this point and are lumped together and given the value necessary to balance the account.

Assuming a nesting success of 60 per cent, including re-nests, which commonly is achieved in Maine, the 12 broods reaching flying age would require 20 original nests. The study area average is 9 eggs per nest; so the 12 successful nests would produce 108 eggs. The observed egg loss is 11 per cent; so only 96 of these eggs hatch. This gives a population made up of 96 ducklings and 24 parents and 16 adults which made up the 8 unsuccessful pairs at the time the broods are hatched.

Juvenile mortality is shown by the brood survival data to be 21 per cent of the ducklings hatched, and in order to balance the account an additional 16 ducks must be lost before October 1. This figure therefore represents the adult mortality from muskrat traps, disease, and predation.

Applying these values in the equation we find that the total of hunting loss, crippling loss, and winter loss is 60 ducks. Hagar (46) reports winter losses on the Massachusetts coast ranging from 10 per cent to 50 per cent of the population remaining after the shooting season; so, assuming a value of 30 per cent for this unknown, it is possible to compute the magnitude of the other two losses as follows:

Winter loss x

Hunting loss ......y

Crippling loss 21%y

then, $x + (y + 21\%y) = 60$

$x + 121\%y = 60$

$x = 60 - 1.21y$

but, $y = 30\%$ of pop. after shooting season,

then, $x = \dfrac{3}{10}(100 - 1.21y)$

so: $\dfrac{3}{10}$ (100—1.21y)=60—1.21y

$$300—3.63y=600—12.1y$$

adding 12.1y to both sides

$$300+8.5y=600$$

$$8.5y=600—300$$
$$=300$$

$$y=\dfrac{300}{8.5}$$

$$=35.5 \text{ Hunting Loss}$$

$$21\%y= \underline{7.4 \text{ Crippling Loss}}$$

$$x=17.3 \text{ Winter Loss}$$

Thus the final form of the life equation table for this population will be as follows:

LIFE EQUATION FOR A STABLE POPULATION OF BLACK DUCKS, II

Date	Item	Gain	Loss	Current Pop.
October 1	Original population			100
	Hunting Loss		35.3	
	Crippling Loss		7.4	
March 1	Winter Loss		17.3	40
April 18	Nesting	108		148
	Egg Loss		12	
May 30	Hatching			136
	Juvenile mortality		20	
	Adult mortality		16	
October 1	Final population			100
Total	....		108	108

This table shows that 35.3 per cent of the original population is harvested in a year with about average winter loss, if the population remains the same the following year. This shows the heavy utilization of the species by gunners and indicates clearly where the greatest single drain on the population lies. Hunting losses and crippling losses are conditioned by the regulations and by weather, but winter losses are conditioned by weather alone, although they may be alleviated by local feeding programs (46).

The fluctuations in the beeding populations noted earlier are due to changes in the total loss suffered from these three variables, which are in turn dependent upon the weather during the hunting season, the weather during late winter, the number of hunters, and the allowable legal take. The only one of these factors within the control of man is the allowable legal take, and it is with this tool alone that we must regulate the greatest single drain on the species. Management must therefore concentrate on developing usable methods of measuring the kill and crippling loss, and on improving the carrying capacity of the winter range to reduce winter loss. These three things are the key to management on the winter range.

On the breeding range and the post-breeding range, the total loss of adults to muskrat traps, spring shooting, disease, and predation is almost equal to the winter loss. As disease is not known to be an important factor in Black Ducks, and spring shooting is slight, the greater part of this loss is due to accidental mortality in muskrat traps and to predation. Predation is to a large extent beyond the control of man, but the removal of the muskrat trap from the important breeding areas in regions of high trapping intensity in southern Canada and the northeastern states by April 1 would be a step of major importance in breeding ground management.

This table also provides an opportunity to approximate nesting densities. It shows that 20 nests are required in the spring to produce 100 ducks in the fall. If a fall census on the study area shows 900 blacks present, there must have been 180 nests that spring. There are approximately 7,000 acres of Black Duck nesting habitat on the area so that the nesting density was 1 nest per 39 acres, and shows clearly why nest hunting for Black Ducks is an unprofitable pursuit in this region.

THE RELATIVE IMPORTANCE OF THE SUB-DIVISIONS OF THE NORTHEASTERN BREEDING GROUNDS

The solution of this important question must await the accumulation of large amounts of banding data, as it is only by this means that we are able to trace a bird from the region where it is hatched to the point where it is shot and makes its contribution to the annual harvest.

A start was made on this problem by the establishment of banding stations at Tinker Harbor on the Labrador coast, at Grand Codroy River in Newfoundland, and at Baie Johan Beetz on the North Shore of the Gulf of St. Lawrence. In 1950, these three original stations were augmented by three more, one in Quebec and two in Ontario, but the new stations have not yet been established long enough to justify any conclusions from their data.

The original three stations have been in operation four years at this writing, and it is possible to draw certain inferences from their results to date. They show that there is considerable overlapping on the winter range of the eastern and western populations. Addy (4) shows that the birds coming south through eastern Ontario winter on the coast with the northeastern population in about equal numbers with those wintering in the Mississippi valley. In other words, no specific area of breeding ground is supplying the bulk of the kill at any of the important shooting grounds such as Cape May, New Jersey. The birds shot there may be bred as far apart as the Labrador coast and the Lake of the Woods in Ontario; thus the main hunting pressure is distributed fairly evenly over the breeding grounds.

Local differences in hunting pressure are discernible, however, from the banding data available. Addy (3) shows that approximately 90 per cent of all recoveries of Newfoundland birds were taken north of Long Island, and that the largest number of recoveries from this population came from the southern tip of Nova Scotia. They also are shot quite heavily in southwestern Newfoundland before they leave for the mainland.

In Nova Scotia and New Brunswick, the local populations are shot heavily at the beginning of the season, which starts in September in some localities. An unusually heavy early kill in New Brunswick is indicated by the fact that 90 per cent of all recoveries were taken during the first fall (3).

The birds from eastern Quebec and Labrador contribute to the harvest all down the coast to Cape Hatteras, with 41 per cent of the recoveries coming from south of Long Island. About half of these recoveries come from southern New Jersey, and it is possible that this region may be their main wintering ground. They show a distinct coastal distribution and do not appear to move inland on the winter range. The birds from western and southern Quebec move southward down the Lake Champlain and Hudson River valleys and winter in the Carolinas. They appear to be a rather distinct population, breeding in the lower St. Lawrence watershed, Vermont, and eastern New York, and they have limited affinities with the maritime populations to the east or the Ontario population to the west.

The Ontario population shows its highest density of banding recoveries from the shores of Lake Erie in Ohio, Michigan, and Ontario. This western population originating in Ontario, New York, and Pennsylvania shows the widest distribution of all with recoveries ranging from the Atlantic coast to the edge of the plains in Kansas. On the coast, this flight begins to mingle with the northeastern population along the eastern shore of Virginia, where they winter in numbers on the inner marshes of Chesapeake Bay.

It might be argued that it is pointless to go back to pre-white-man days and compare conditions on the flyway then and now. We know that conditions over the continent have changed drastically for wildlife and that it never will be possible to restore the conditions of that time. This argument holds good for almost all parts of the continent but the one we are discussing. The northern breeding grounds of the Black Duck are today, with the exception of changes in the plant succession, which are very slow in this region, the same as they were on that long-forgotten day when Lief, son of Eric the Red, made his famous landfall somewhere on the coast between Nova Scotia and Labrador in the year 1,000, and we have seen that the waterfowl spend almost two-thirds of their lives in this great unchanged region. Therefore, it seems fair to assume that the long-term downward trend in the population is due to changes on the southern part of the flyway where man has made himself felt.

It will be of interest here to describe briefly the history of the white man's influence on the northern breeding grounds, and to note his effect upon this great and still little-known region. Before 1630 the Eskimos inhabited the whole of the Labrador coast and the eastern part of the North Shore of the Gulf of St. Lawrence. During that year the Indians were armed by the French and attacked the Eskimos and drove them north, and today they do not travel farther south than Hamilton Inlet on the Labrador coast. Until as late as 1821, the only trading post in the interior was at Lake Mistassini in the southwest corner of the country at the head of the Rupert River. The supplies for the post were transported by *voyageurs* from James Bay.

Between 1821-1824, James Clouston was employed by the amalgamated Hudson's Bay Company and the Northwest Company in exploring the country east of Hudson Bay, and Low (*Ibid.*) says, "The country was explored and posts established throughout the interior." However, he does not mention where any of these posts were and how far the exploration was carried into the central plateau. Three years later, in 1827, Dr. Mendry coasted along the east shore of Richmond Gulf and crossed overland through the Clearwater and Seal Lakes to the Larch branch of the Koksoak and down to the present site of Fort Chimo. He established the post in that year, and this trip is the basis for the famous boys' book, Ballantyne's "Ungava."

In January and February, 1863, John McLean crossed overland to Hamilton Inlet from Fort Chimo and returned by the same route, reaching Chimo on the return trip on April 20. The same year a post was established at Erlandson's Lake, which seems to have been on the headwaters of the Whale River, and another post also was established on the George. In 1840, Fort Nascaupee was established on Lake Petitsikapau, and Erlandson's Lake was abandoned.

By 1857, the maximum number of posts were in operation in the interior. They were Mistassini, Temiskami, Lake St. John, all in the extreme southwest corner of the region; and Waswanipi, Mechiskan, Pike Lake, Nichicun, Kaniapiskau and Fort Nascaupee in the remainder. The whole Ungava district was closed from 1842 to 1866, but in the latter year Fort Chimo was reopened. The reason for the closing of the posts can be surmised from the contents of the following letter. William Kennedy of Fort Chimo, writing to the council of the Hudson's Bay Company in the winter of 1851, says: "Starvation has, I learn, committed great havoc among our old friends the Nascaupees, numbers of whom met their deaths from want last winter; whole camps of them were found dead, without one survivor to tell the tale of their sufferings." (70)

The reason for this disaster was the failure of the caribou migration, and one of the main reasons why the caribou shifted their range can be deduced from Low's (pp. 413) description of the state of the interior range. "At least half of the forest area of the interior has been totally destroyed by fire within the past 25-30 years . . . The greatest fire of modern times . . . swept the country south of the height-of-land from the St. Maurice to beyond the Romaine (1870-1871) . . . The Nascaupee Indians of the semibarrens signal one another by smoke made by burning the white lichens that cover most of the ground in the interior, and these signals cause many fires . . . fires accidentally made, or set on purpose by owners of schooners, who often fire the country along the shore, so as to easily make dry firewood for future seasons." The lichens consumed in these fires are slow growing, and they constitute the major food of the caribou. It is only fair to the Indians to add, however, that recent work in this region has shown that many fires are started by lightning.

By 1873, starvation had so reduced the Indians, and consequently their fur catch, that Fort Nascaupee was abandoned, and the following year Michikamau Post also closed. This left only Nichicun, Mistassini, and Waswanipi in the interior. Twenty years later, starvation struck again on the Koksoak, and more than 150 persons of the 350 in the Koksoak band died during the winter of 1893-1894. Starvation also was rampant on the Eastmain, and Low passed Indian camps with everything in order on the bank of the river when he passed down in the spring, but with not one survivor left. He concluded that "the highest estimate of the Indian population of the Labrador Peninsula does not exceed 3,500 and is more likely nearer 3,000." The total population of the peninsula in 1895, including whites and Eskimos, was 14,300, or one to 35 square miles. The Canadian Department of Indian Affairs estimated the Indian population at 4,648 in 1924, which works out at 125 square miles for each Indian, and about 500 square miles for every hunter (28).

In 1912, Fort Nichicun, or Nitchequon as it is now called, was closed due to the rising costs of supplying this far-distant post from Rupert's House on James Bay. A new post was opened 150 miles nearer the coast to take care of the Nitchequon trade, but in 1939 the old post was reopened at a new locality on the same lake.

The first modern surveys of the interior were made by the Canadian geologist, A. P. Low, whose report is the basis of much of the information given here. He explored and mapped the main rivers of the region, and his description was the best picture we had of some of the remote interior districts until they were photographed from the air in World War II. The south-north traverse was run in 1917 by an expedition from the Carnegie Museum of Pittsburgh under W. E. C. Todd, and the north-south trip was made by a Hudson's Bay Company post manager and his wife from Chimo.

With the re-establishment of Nitchequon post and Fort McKenzie on the Koksoak, there now are bands of Indians who remain in the interior the year 'round, but natives from the Gulf of St. Lawrence posts travel far into the interior and may trade one year at North West River, another year at Fort Chimo, and the third year back at Mingan. The well known canoe routes of the interior are all along main watercourses, and these nomadic wanderers criss-cross the peninsula in their travels to and from their hunting grounds in spring and fall.

About 1930 prospectors became interested in the country about the headwaters of the Hamilton River, and in 1938 the Labrador Mining and Exploration Company obtained a concession to 18,000 square miles on the Labrador side of the Quebec-Labrador boundary. Three years later the Hollinger Consolidated Gold Mines Limited took over this concession and began exploring both sides of the border. In the spring of 1945 the company's chief geologist reported nine high-grade iron ore bodies discovered in Labrador and 15 in Ungava.

Hollinger now has a 20-year exclusive concession to explore and develop 3,900 square miles of Ungava territory directly across the border from its Labrador holdings. The company plans to build a railway to this area from Seven Islands on the Gulf of St. Lawrence, and construction was started in 1950.

The most recent development in this little-known area was the discovery, in 1950, of what may be the largest meteorite crater in the world. This curious circular lake seven and one-half miles around and two and one-quarter miles wide, rimmed by 500-foot high cliffs and ripples in the granite plain 60 feet high, was discovered in the extreme northwestern tip of the peninsula by a prospector studying aerial photographs. This whole area was photographed from the air during World War II, since it lies on the fighter staging route to Europe, and every square mile now can be examined for the first time. This, of course, is of great help to the prospector, who now can locate likely areas in the hinterland of

Ungava from his head office in Toronto, but it also enables the game manager better to assess the ground he is studying, which he could not cover in a lifetime on foot or by canoe.

It will be seen that from the end of the Ice Age to about 1930 the white man's influence on the northern breeding ground of the Black Duck was negligible. With the arrival of the prospector and the survey crews, the primitive era began to draw to a close, and from 1950 onward, the steel rails pushing northward from Seven Islands will seal the doom of the wilderness solitude that has held sway in this region since before the first men came. It seems, therefore, that the interior breeding grounds will not remain inviolate for long, and as the construction crews increase and mining camps develop and push farther and farther into the wilderness, the already sparse wildlife of the region will be subjected to added hunting pressure, not from primitive hunters hunting to feed their families, but from white men with plenty of ammunition and modern guns who are dissatisfied with camp grub, or who want to hunt for recreation. When to this burden is added the mobility of the airplane, which can drop a party of hunters at any of the innumerable lakes of the back country to stay for a day or a month, it can be appreciated that the Black Duck's main stronghold has lost forever its greatest asset, inaccessibility.

On the credit side of the ledger, the new railway will enable biologists to study the wildlife problems of the region in a manner never before possible, and it will open up great areas to possible management by stocking and habitat improvement. It also will carry law enforcement to the remote camps of the interior.

In an area of over 600,000 square miles no management was needed until the approach of civilization brought modern man and his unequalled destructive capacity into the picture. As this is being written that approach is going forward spike by spike, and we who are interested in the perpetuation of waterfowl in the Atlantic flyway must learn to think about the Labrador-Ungava country as the midwestern does about the northern prairie provinces. It is an important waterfowl producing area which is being opened for the first time.

Wildlife management in this area will be concerned first with the provision of adequate food supplies for the natives, and only after this has been assured will the management of sport species be considered seriously. Rousseau (107) already has recommended the introduction of reindeer and mountain goats into the George River drainage to augment the meat supply provided now entirely by the badly depleted native caribou, and Hustich (59) and Polunin (100) have given the basic phytogeographical information upon which broad management areas can be drawn.

The most promising areas for waterfowl management probably will lie in the valleys of the Kaniapiskau and the Hamilton, as there the best soils are to be found. Precambrian sedimentary rocks are dominant in the Koksoak-Kaniapiskau valley, and balsam fir, balsam poplar and white birch are fairly common. The bedrock of the Hamilton valley often is of sedimentary origin and intrusive rocks richer in calcium than the usual granite-gneiss of the interior occur. The bulk of the nesting population can be expected to be found in the boreal forest region of the south and in the taiga region across the center of the peninsula, with the forest-tundra and the barrens being the least productive.

Another potentially important area is the region of large marshes at the headwaters of the Eagle, Paradise and St. Lewis rivers south of the Mealy Mountains in southeastern Labrador. These marshes are several thousand square miles in area, and they were examined by an ornothologist for the first time in 1950. Addy and Cool of the U. S. Fish and Wildlife Service flew over them and landed on several of the lakes. The waterfowl population seen was not large and consisted mainly of moulting Black Ducks, and these were assembled on some of the larger lakes of the region. A few broods were seen, and these authors comment that brood survival might be exceedingly low because of the large numbers of great northern pike in the shallow lakes and streams. The habitat is a series of many shallow ponds and streams through open marshes and muskegs of the acid-bog type, and the principal aquatic plant noted was the yellow pondlily, *Nuphar*, (136). The introduction of food plants for acid habitats, such as ribbonleaf and floating leaf pondweed and watershield, and screening streams for pike control might have possibilities there when management of these remote areas becomes possible.

THE POSSIBILITIES FOR BREEDING GROUND MANAGEMENT

Breeding ground management in eastern Canada can take the form of improving the carrying capacity of habitat already in use, or of introducing breeders into existing habitats which are not in use. As it is doubtful if there are many areas in this region where the habitat already is crowded to capacity with breeding ducks, the latter form of management would seem to hold the greatest possibilities. Snyder (112) tells of the success attained by introducing a mongrel flock of Black Ducks into an unoccupied habitat near Toronto in 1931. These birds became established and attracted numbers of wild blacks and Mallards, and now hundreds of these ducks winter in the Toronto area, and many nest along the banks of the nearby rivers and lakes. He also points out that there may be innumerable situations in the northeast where Black Ducks could exist now but where there is no tradition of tenure to fill them. The locating and filling of these vacant ecological niches is the key to breeding ground management.

When it is appreciated that in the Province of Quebec alone there are over 8,000 leased lakes and 200 leased rivers for hunting and fishing purposes, and that most of these belong to well-organized clubs, it becomes apparent that the skeleton organization necessary for a large-scale stocking program is in existence already. Surveys could be made of these properties to determine the suitable habitat, and Black Duck eggs gathered from adjacent habitats could be incubated and the ducklings pen-reared and conditioned to the habitat after release. The work of McCabe (73) with Wood Ducks in

Wisconsin, and Valikangas (133) with Mallards in Finland indicates that a proportion would return to the place where they learned to fly. Stocking projects of this kind in New York, coupled with development of small marshes, have resulted in production as high as 5 blacks and Wood Ducks per acre (17).

The chances of success of such plants would appear to be greater if they were made of young females only. Of 95 Black Ducks retrapped at the same station on succeeding years, 64 per cent were females, and of 68 retrapped the first year after banding, 63 per cent were females. As the young females pair on the winter range the first year, the lack of males planted in the areas to be stocked would have no significance, and the expense of transportation and conditioning to the habitat would be limited to the birds that could be expected to return. The young males could be released at the assembly points in the region as soon as they were old enough to fend for themselves.

Such a program would require a central hatchery from which the ducklings would be shipped to the selected areas for release. They should be kept in a pen at the site of the release until old enough to band, and all banding and sex and age data should be recorded carefully. These data will yield valuable information on survival at a later date. Procuring an adequate supply of eggs in the wild will present considerable problems, and it may be necessary to resort to game farm stock of proven quality for at least part of the original plant. The undesirable features of this procedure will be kept to a minimum if the female only is released as she will mate with a wild male, and her blood lines soon will be bred out in favor of the local stock.

One such hatchery would serve the requirements for stocking projects in the whole breeding range of the Black Duck from Newfoundland to Ontario and could be supported on a cooperative basis by the sportsmen's organizations and provinces of the region, and by international conservation organizations.

As winter range management is going forward now to adjust the deficiencies caused by marsh drainage for mosquito control, which ruined many acres of winter range; by hurricanes, which drastically altered the vegetation of many marshes and filled others completely; and by the constant pressure of increased human population with its attendant demand for summer cottages on the seashore, the time has come for a program of breeding ground management to go hand-in-hand with winter range management. Such a program could combine the stocking projects outlined above with the marsh management methods outlined by Mendall (81), which were so successful in Maine, and by Addy and MacNamara (2).

The stabilization of water levels on selected marsh areas, where the majority of the breeding ducks nest in the marshes, together with the provision of food, by planting if necessary, and adequate territorial facilities, are the key to successful management of individual marshes in the northeast. This system raised the breeding population of a Maine marsh from 4 to 14 pairs of blacks on about 70 acres, which is a high nesting density for that region. The success of that experiment indicates that many club properties in Quebec and other Canadian provinces may be capable of being developed to produce more blacks. The cost of the Maine development was slightly more than $200; so such developments would be well within the budget of many clubs.

A third, but definitely inferior form of management, is to introduce a buffer species into the range of the east coast flight. There is no satisfactory buffer species to absorb some of the shooting now directed at the blacks between Quebec and Delaware, and the successful introduction of Mallards undoubtedly would take some of the pressure off the blacks. But such an introduction would only offer competition for food, and areas suitable for planting Mallards also are suitable for planting blacks; so, if the stocking program mentioned above is undertaken, there would be no reason to introduce a second species. The available habitat then could be stocked directly, and the need for a buffer would diminish as the population increased and became better able to stand the shooting pressure.

An extensive program of small marsh development already is underway in the northeastern States. Maine, Massachusetts, New Jersey, Rhode Island, Maryland and Delaware along the coastal strip, and Vermont and New Hampshire farther inland all have marshes of various sizes under management for waterfowl. The most outstanding program is farther west, however, in the State of New York. In 1953, New York had 498 small marshes developed with a total area of about 2,500 acres. They varied in size from 1 to 70 acres, but the average was between 4 and 5 acres. In addition, another 400 potholes of $\frac{1}{5}$ acres each were planned for early development.

The cost of this work in New York is estimated at $200 per marsh acre, but that includes the efforts of the wildlife manager in selling the program as well as all surveys and development. In Canada, this figure should be considerably less.

The opinions on the future of the program differ in the various states as their topographical features vary. In New York the future looks bright, but the cost of maintenance of these areas still is unknown. In Maine there are tremendous possibilities for the development of marshes and tidal estuaries, but the program is just starting. In Massachusetts the program is again in its infancy and is expected to expand. In New Jersey the emphasis is on the development of larger marshes as they are not shot out so easily as small marshes. This is important in a state with heavy gun pressure. Rhode Island is optimistic about the future, and Maryland has extensive possibilities along the Chesapeake Bay coastal area on the Eastern Shore. When the marsh owners become aware of the possibilities of developing their land for waterfowl and muskrats many requests for technical assistance are expected.

In Delaware, the possibilities of small marsh development are limited as most sites are subject to tidal action. Small areas of improvement in larger marshes may be the solution there. In the mountainous regions of New Hampshire, such a program also has limited possibilities and probably will be restricted to the more open agricultural areas. In the State of Vermont, the Champlain valley offers the greatest possibilities, and some large marshes already are under management. A start has been made with the development of small marshes, and it is hoped that the program will sell itself when the demonstration areas come into full production.

Banding has been carried on intermittently for many years in the southern breeding grounds of the Black Duck, but our knowledge of the importance of many areas is far from complete, and a larger and better coordinated banding program is needed badly. No banding has been done north of Hamilton Inlet on the Atlantic coast, and none north of the southern end of James Bay in the Hudson Bay drainage. Even in the southern areas, our knowledge is not complete. A banding station is needed badly on the St. Lawrence between Pointe des Monts and the Island of Orleans to show where the birds from the St. Lawrence, which migrate up the river, cross to the Atlantic coast. This is an important flight which provides most of the duck shooting for the Quebec gunners and is the breeding stock of the western half of that province.

The banding of young birds before they can fly yields valuable information for the management of local populations, and is a field of endeavor which hardly has been touched in this northeastern region. Where are the birds bred in your marsh being shot? The only way to find out is to band them before their primaries develop and you are sure they have not flown in from elsewhere. Then you can follow the returns and see just where they are being taken. This type of information is vital to management and can be obtained only by a concerted effort on the part of the interested parties. Non-flying young Black Ducks are scattered so widely that large numbers cannot be captured at one time, the same as the young of the concentrated nesters of the west. Therefore, the work must be conducted year after year in the same area to build up a usable number of returns gradually.

Another management practice for this region is to take the

muskrat trapper out of the major breeding areas by April 1, in regions of intensive trapping. These regions are the northern tier of states, the southern counties of Ontario and Quebec, and the Maritime provinces. Some provinces and states have abolished spring muskrat trapping already, but it should be brought to the attention of those who have not that it is a management measure for the good of all, as waterfowl are no respecters of political boundaries.

Finally, the accumulation of accurate data by teams of trained wildlife biologists on hunter kill and crippling loss should be organized in a uniform manner to cover the major shooting areas of the region. This work should be done as a cooperative effort between the Provincial and Federal departments, with private organizations assisting where possible.

None of these measures is beyond our capabilities today, and if a serious effort is to be made to manage the Black Duck population so that the hunter may get a maximum return when a "high tide and an east wind" set the stage for him, action must be taken to implement them.

Such is the story of the Black Duck on its breeding grounds in eastern Canada. Many things still remain to be learned; but a start has been made, and a definite course of action seems indicated. The next step is to apply these findings on the land.

Appendix I.

NESTING DATES OF BLACK DUCKS

Date Found	Nests	Eggs	Location	Reported By	Remarks
March 15	1	..	Grand Manan Islands, N. B.	Peters	
April 18-June 19	6	..	New York	Bent	
April 20-May 10	several	..	Maryland and Virginia	Bent	
April 23	1	..	Basque Island, Quebec	Provancher Society	
April 23	1	..	Migic, N. B.	Peters	
April 23-June 2	7	..	Massachusetts and Rhode Island	Bent	
April 25-July 3	8	..	New Jersey	Bent	
April 30-June 28	54	..	Ontario, Quebec, Nova Scotia	Bent	
May 3	1	8	Study Area, N. B.	Wright	
May 3	1	9	Study Area, N. B.	Wright	Tree
May 3	1	8	Study Area, N. B.	Wright	
May 3	1	..	Study Area, N. B.	Peters	
May 9	1	4	Study Area, N. B.	Wright	Tree
May 10	1	11	Prince Edward Island	Wright	
May 12	1	3	Study Area, N. B.	Wright	Tree
May 13	1	9	Study Area, N. B.	Wright	
May 14	1	..	Jolicure, N. B.	Peters	
May 14	1	8	Havre St. Pierre, Quebec	Lewis	
May 18	1	9	Cronk Lake, N. B.	Wright	
May 18	1	5	Study Area, N. B.	Wright	Tree
May 20	1	..	Montreal, Quebec	Mousley	
May 22	1	12	New Jersey	Bent	
May 23	..	..	Upper Hamilton River, Labrador	Low	
May 23	1	9	Islands off the Maine coast	Gross	
May 26	1	8	Study Area, N. B.	Wright	Tree
May 28	1	..	Sandwich Bay, Labrador	Austin	
June 11	1	9	Islands off the Maine coast	Gross	
June 12	1	7	Islands off the Maine coast	Gross	
June 17	1	..	Fox Pond, Pennsylvania	Todd	
June 18	1	..	Study Area, N. B.	Wright	
June 21	1	..	Magdalen Islands, Quebec	Bent	
June 23	1	..	Magdalen Islands, Quebec	Bent	
TOTAL	101 plus				

Appendix II.

Predation Data

PREDATION–DUCKLING

Kill No.	Date	Place	Prey Species	Evidence	Predator
1	7/1/46	Musquash Is. Queens Co., N. B.	Black Duck, ¾ grown.	Imm. Bald Eagle seen leaving perch under which kill was found. Body plucked and cleaned out. Wings, legs and back not touched. Head cleaned out.	Bald Eagle, Immature
2	8/20/46	Tabusintac, Gloucester Co., N. B.	Black Duck, ¾ grown.	Primaries and scapulars clipped. Feathers not scattered. Wing bones chewed. Fox scat present. Date of kill: before mid-July as primaries were not yet fully developed.	Fox
3	9/4/46	Study Area	Wood Duck, ¾ grown.	Marsh Hawk flushed from kill by H. Mendall.	Marsh Hawk
4	9/5/46	Musquash Is. Queens Co., N. B.	Black Duck, ¾ grown.	Primaries and breast feathers found under same perch as #1. Two Bald Eagles flying over perch. Also present 3 pickerel heads and remains of unidentified fish.	Bald Eagle
5	9/13/46	Lake St. Peter, P. Q.	Black Duck, ½ grown.	One wing joined to body. All bones present. Skull broken in, bill separated. Wing showing pin feathers only. Red-tailed Hawk primary present. No flesh remaining. Est. age of kill–1 month.	Red-Tailed Hawk
6	6/16/49	Study Area	Black Duck, ¼ grown.	Duckling found weak but alive with tip of bill bitten off cleanly and tongue protruding. Unable to dive. Duckling collected.	Snapping Turtle
7	6/20/49	Study Area	Black Duck, ¼ grown.	Duckling pulled under and released. Picked up bleeding and died in hand. Many teeth marks.	Pickerel or Eel

One leg amputated and ... although duckling still in the down.

PREDATION–NEST

Kill No.	Date	Place	Prey Species	Evidence	Predator
1	6/1/46	Study Area	Black Duck Tree Nest	Characteristic punctures and crows seen about the nest.	Crow
2	6/27/46	Study Area	Black Duck Tree Nest	Eggs crushed and contents lapped. Membrane sticking to inside of shell.	Raccoon
3	7/5/46	Lakeville Corner, Sunbury Co., N. B.	B. W. Teal incubating female	Head torn off but body not eaten. Farmer blames his cat.	Domestic Cat
4	Approx. 6/7/47	Lakeville Corner, Sunbury Co., N. B.	B. W. Teal	One egg out of 11 left near nest. Half shell only, no bill puncture.	Unident. Mammal
5	6/18/47	Study Area	Black Duck	Two eggs found in open field showing bill punctures.	Crow
6	5/26/48	Study Area	Black Duck Tree Nest	Young Female Raccoon caught in act of robbing nest. 8 eggs destroyed.	Raccoon
7	7/8/48	Study Area	Com. Loon	The single egg destroyed and eaten with characteristic puncture. Crows seen near nest.	Crow
8	5/11/49	Study Area	Black Duck Ground Nest	Nest partially destroyed. 8 eggs removed without a trace.	Unknown
9	5/31/49	Study Area	Black Duck Tree Nest	Female killed on nest and 9 eggs eaten. Feathers clipped, body eaten. Vertebrae chewed at base of skull. Body left at foot of tree.	Raccoon
10	6/3/49	Study Area	Black Duck Tree Nest	Eggs in water at foot of tree showing punctures.	Crow

PREDATION—ADULT

Kill No.	Date	Place	Prey Species	Evidence	Predator
1	7/18/46	Study Area	Adult Black Duck	Kill on log 15 yds. from water. Wings present, feathers not clipped. Body feathers not scattered. Body ripped open and viscera eaten. Bones not chewed. Head missing. Droppings suggest scavenging by crow. Body feathers under new growth of ferns, i.e., kill one month old.	Unident. Raptor
2	8/3/46	Study Area	Unident. Adult Black Duck	Bald Eagle seen carrying duck.	Bald Eagle
3	8/23/46	Bloom Point, P.E.I.	Adult Black Duck	Feathers clipped. Body present and mostly eaten. Head and neck severed. Bones chewed. Fox scat present. One week old.	Fox
4	8/25/46	Kamouraska, P. Q.	Black Duck	Wings present. Feathers plucked in bunches. Bones not broken. Body plucked. One leg and part of another eaten. Two weeks old. Found on open ground.	Unident. Raptor
5	9/10/46	Study Area	Black Duck	One scapular of Black Duck found under Eagle feeding perch. Body not found.	Bald Eagle
6	9/10/46	Study Area	Black Duck	Black Duck feathers under eagle feeding perch (not same perch as #5). Three Imm. Bald Eagle seen to leave the perch.	Bald Eagle
7	11/1/46	Grand Lake, N. B.	Scaup	On lake shore. Feathers clipped, body carried away. Probably cripple as in heavily shot area.	Unident. Mammal

	Date	Location	Species	Remarks	Predator
0	6/10/47	Study Area	Unident. Duck	Bald Eagle seen to swoop on pond at hind fringe of alders. Loud frantic quacking was heard and the eagle rose carrying an unident. duck.	Bald Eagle
9	11/14/47	Washdamoak Lake, N. B.	Unident. Duck	Adult Bald Eagle seen to dive and pick up unident. duck from area where three cripples were lost that morning.	Bald Eagle
10	11/15/47	Forshay's Lake, N. B.	Black Duck	Feathers clipped. Fox scats present. Probably cripple as area heavily shot.	Fox
11	5/7/48	Oromocto Is. N. B.	Wood Duck	Feathers at mouth of occupied fox den.	Fox
12	5/11/48	Oromocto Is. N. B.	Ring-Neck Duck Female	Wing and body feathers at mouth of occupied fox den.	Fox
13	8/3/49	Study Area	Wood Duck, Immature	Feathers on water under perch plucked out in bunches.	Unident. Raptor
14	8/3/49	Study Area	Black Duck, Immature	Feathers clipped on edge of slough. Body carried off. Duck apparently killed when sleeping on bank. Flightless ducks in the area.	Fox
15	8/9/49	Study Area	Unident. Duck	Feathers plucked under perch overhanging water. Body carried away.	Unident. Raptor
16	8/15/49	Study Area	Ring-Neck Duck, Adult Female	Feathers plucked under tall stump. Body carried away; blood on stump.	Unident. Raptor
	8/4/49		Black Duck	*Negative Evidence* Marsh Hawk flew over 3 Black Ducks only 3 feet above them, and they paid no attention to it. Hawk swooped and soared very near them, but paid no attention to the ducks.	Marsh Hawk

Appendix III

Waterfowl Food Habits Studies
Ungava Bay to the Bay of Fundy

1. WATERFOWL FOODS OF FALSE RIVER, UNGAVA BAY

(Stomach analyses by Dr. A. C. Martin.)

Species	No. Stomachs	% Animal	% Vegetable
Black Duck	8	35	65
Pintail	13	2	98
G-w Teal	9	—	100
Old Squaw	2	25	75
R-b Merganser	2	58	42
Can. Goose	2	—	100
Total	37	—	—

Black Duck 8 Stomachs August 23-26

Food Item	% Total	% Total
Vegetable		
Empetraceae.		47
Crowberry (Empetrum nigrum)	47	
Cyanophyceae.		18
Filamentous Algae.	18	
Araliaceae.		Tr
Marestail (Hippuris vulgaris)	Tr	
Ericaceae.		Tr
Blueberry, cranberry (Vaccinium sp.)	Tr	
Bearberry (Arctostaphylos uvaursi)	Tr	
Vegetable Fibers.		Tr
Total Vegetable Food		65%
Animal		
Gastropoda.		24
Snail fragments (probably Littoria obstusata)	24	
Amphipoda.		11
Amphipod (Gammarus)	11	
Cladocera.		Tr
Daphnia type	Tr	
Total Animal Food		35%

2. BLACK DUCK FOODS OF TINKER HARBOR, LABRADOR
10 Stomachs Aug. 17-Sept. 22

Food Item	% Total (Excl. gravel)
Vegetable	
Veg. fibers.	43
Empetraceae.	
Crowberry (Empetrum nigrum)	11
Carex.	
Sedge	1
Total Veg. Food	55%
Animal	
Amphipoda.	
Orchestia grillus	29
Gastropoda.	
Broken snail shells	16
Total Animal Food	45%

3. BLACK DUCK FOODS OF BAIE JOHAN BEETZ, P. Q. THE NORTH SHORE OF THE GULF OF ST. LAWRENCE
14 Stomachs Aug. 13-Oct. 20

Food Item	% Total	% Total (Excl. gravel)
Vegetable		
Nymphaeae.		12
Cowlily (Nuphar rubrodisca).	12	
Najadaceae.		4
Eelgrass (Zostera marina).	3	
Wigeongrass (Ruppia maritima).	1	
Pondweed (Potmogeton epihydrus).	Tr	
Cyperaceae.		4
Sedge (Carex sp.).	4	
Spikerush (Eleocharis palustris).	Tr	
Araceae.		4
Water Arum (Calla palustris).	4	
Sparganiaceae.		1
Burreed (Sparganium sp.).	1	
Gentianaceae.		1
Buckbean (Menyanthes trifoliata).	1	
Unidentified Vegetable fibers.		50
Total Vegetable Food		76%

Animal

Insecta.		10
Miscellaneous insect fragments.	10	
Pelecypoda.		6
Little Blue Mussel.	6	
Gastropoda.		3
Saltwater snails.	3	
Broken shell.		1
Total Animal Food		20%

4. BLACK DUCK FOODS OF THE ST. JOHN VALLEY, N. B.
23 Stomachs July 23-October 8

Food Item	% Total	% Total (Excl. gravel)
Vegetable		
Gramineae.		36
Wildrice (Zizania aquatica).	36	
Cyperaceae.		10
Sedge (Carex sp.).	8	
(Carex Tuckermani).	1	
Torrey's Three-Square Bulrush.		
(Scirpus Tuckermani).	Tr	
Hard-stemmed and Soft-stemmed		
Bulrush (Scirpus acutus and S.		
validus).	Tr	
River Bulrush (S. fluviatilis).	1	
Spikerush (Eleocharis palustris).	Tr	
Najadaceae.		16
Floating-leaved Pondweed (Potamoge-ton natans).	12	
Celery-leaved Pondweed (P. epihydrus).	3	
Variable Pondweed (P. gramineus).	1	
Pondweed (P. pusillus).	Tr	
Pondweed (P. sp.).	Tr	
Sparganiaceae.		8
Burreed (Sparganium sp.).	8	
Alismaceae.		1
Arrowhead (Saggittaria latifolia).	1	
Miscellaneous Veg. Foods.		Tr
Buckbean (Menyanthes trifoliata).	Tr	
Smartweed (Polygonium natans).	Tr	
Bramble (Rubus sp.).	Tr	
Unidentified Veg. Matter.		24
Total Vegetable Food		95%

Animal

Gastropoda.		4
Miscellaneous snails.	4	
Insecta.		1
Miscellaneous insects.	1	
Total Animal Food		5%

5. BLACK DUCK FOODS OF THE BAY OF FUNDY SHORE, N. B.
4 Stomachs Dec. 19-29

Food Item	% Total	% Total (Excl. Gravel)
Animal		
Amphipoda.		69
Gammarus	69	
Pelecypoda.		17
Little Blue Mussel (Mytilus)	17	
Broken Shell.		9
Gastropoda.		5
Periwinkle (Littorina sp.).	5	
Total Animal Food		100%
Vegetable		
Smartwood (Polygonium natans)		Tr
Lead Shot.		Tr

Appendix IV.

Black Duck Fall Weights, New Brunswick & Quebec

Age & Sex	No. Weighed	Avr. Wt. Lbs.	Wt. Range Lbs.
Ad Male	27	2.81	2.25-4.00
Imm Male	53	2.41	1.75-2.75
Ad Female	35	2.55	2.00-3.00
Imm Female	32	2.30	2.00-3.00
Total	147		
Average		2.50	1.75-4.00

The "five-pound" Black Duck sometimes referred to by hunters was not encountered in the course of this study. The largest specimen weighed was a very large adult male shot at Victor Bay, Saguenay County, Quebec, on October 20, 1946, and it weighed an even four pounds. This was one of the late migrating adult males in full winter plumage, a typical specimen of the "northern red-leg."

Appendix V.

The same-season returns of Black Ducks banded in the major flights leaving Canada are shown on the following maps (from Addy 3). From east to west these banding stations are located at the mouth of the Grand Codroy River in Newfoundland; at Tinker Harbor on the Labrador coast; at Baie Johan Beetz on the North Shore of the Gulf of St. Lawrence; in the Lake Champlain country; at Lake Scugog in southeastern Ontario; and at Munuscong in the northern peninsula of Michigan.

All of these ducks were banded in the period June-December and were recovered during the same period or during the following January, i.e. in the hunting season of the same year. Local recoveries were considered to be those taken within 50 miles of the banding station.

Charts

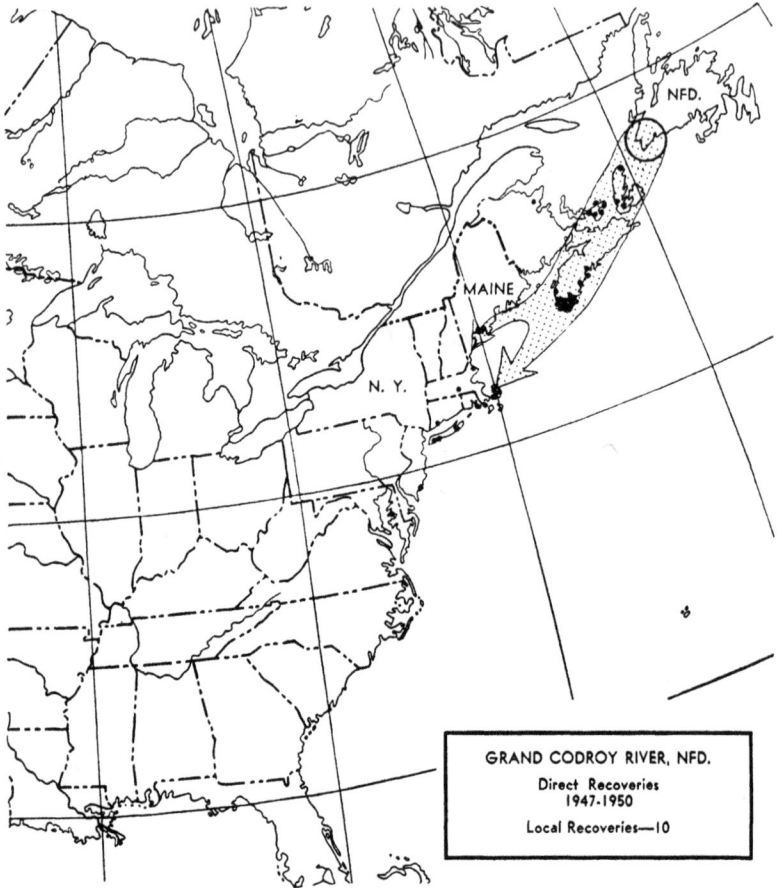

GRAND CODROY RIVER, NFD.

Direct Recoveries
1947-1950

Local Recoveries—10

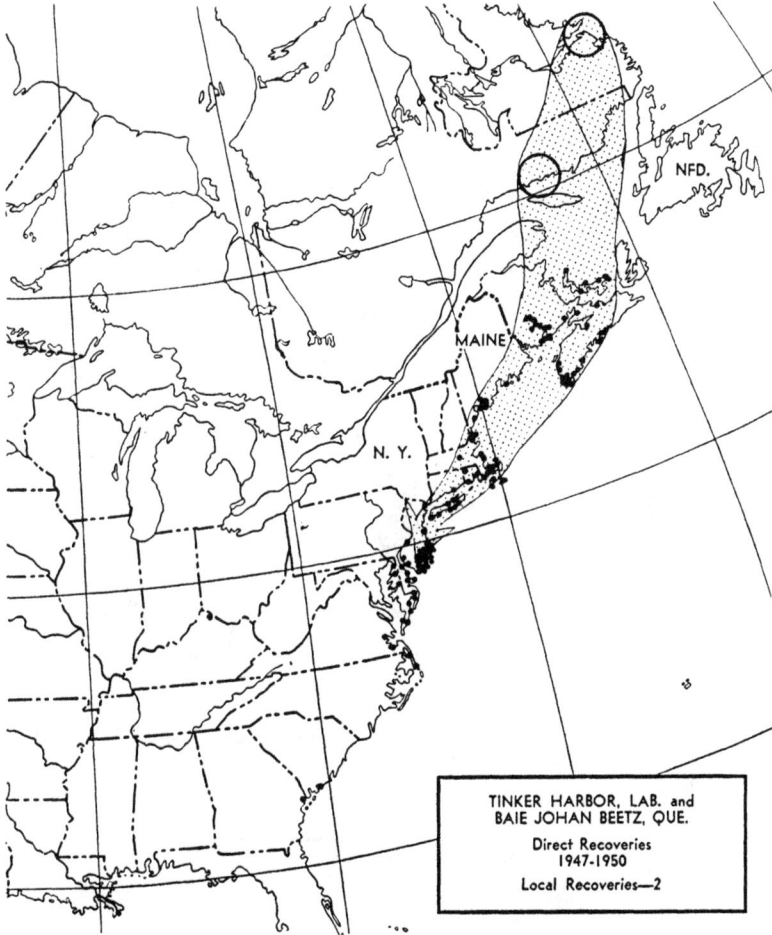

TINKER HARBOR, LAB. and
BAIE JOHAN BEETZ, QUE.

Direct Recoveries
1947-1950

Local Recoveries—2

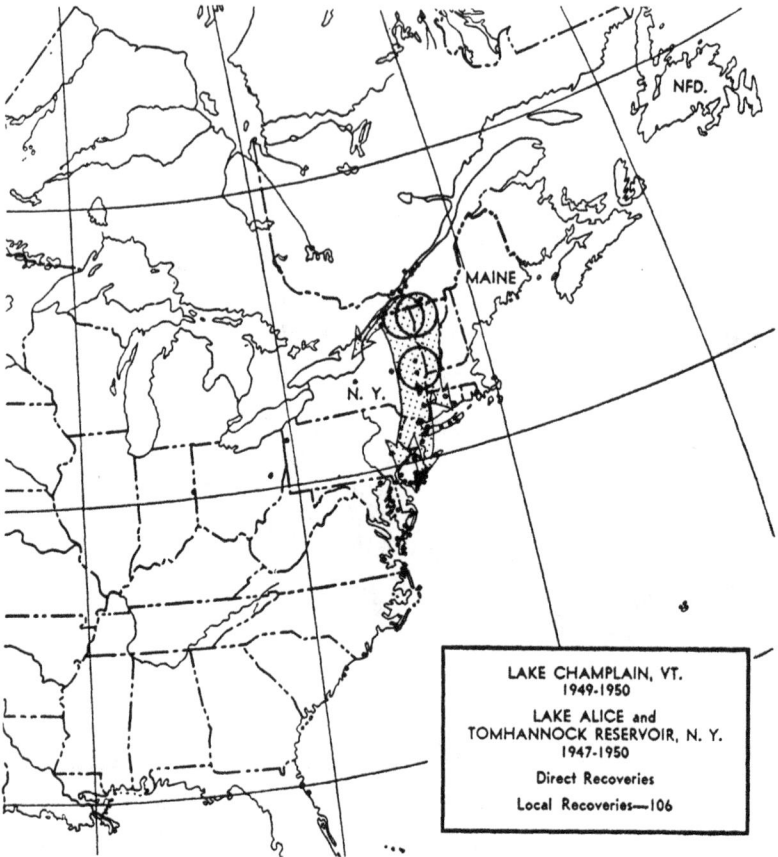

LAKE CHAMPLAIN, VT.
1949-1950

LAKE ALICE and
TOMHANNOCK RESERVOIR, N. Y.
1947-1950

Direct Recoveries

Local Recoveries—106

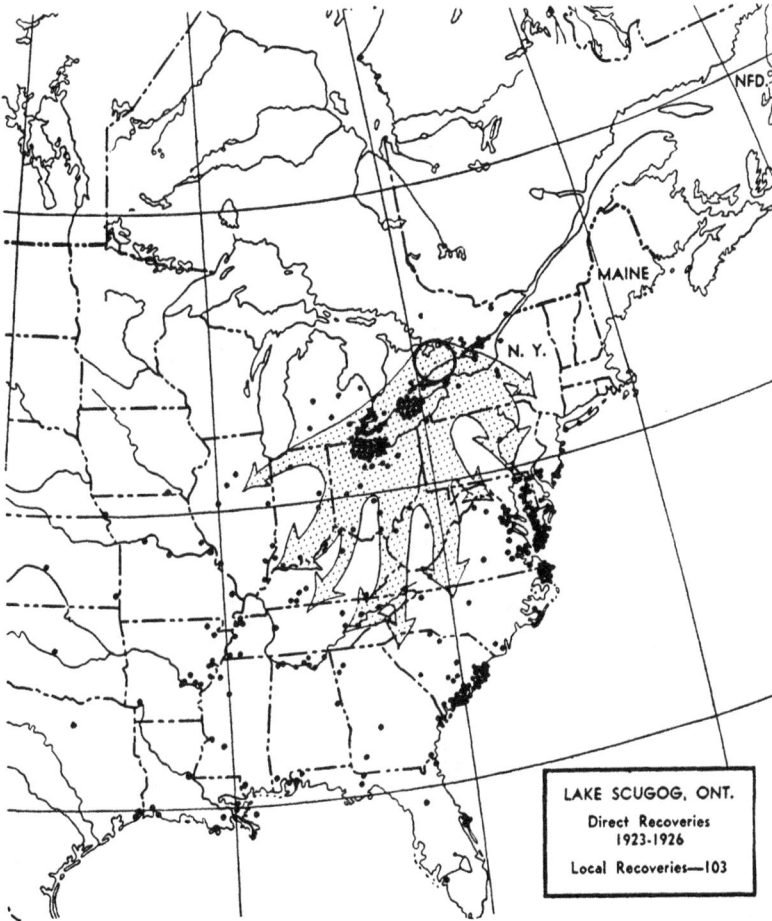

LAKE SCUGOG, ONT.

Direct Recoveries
1923-1926

Local Recoveries—103

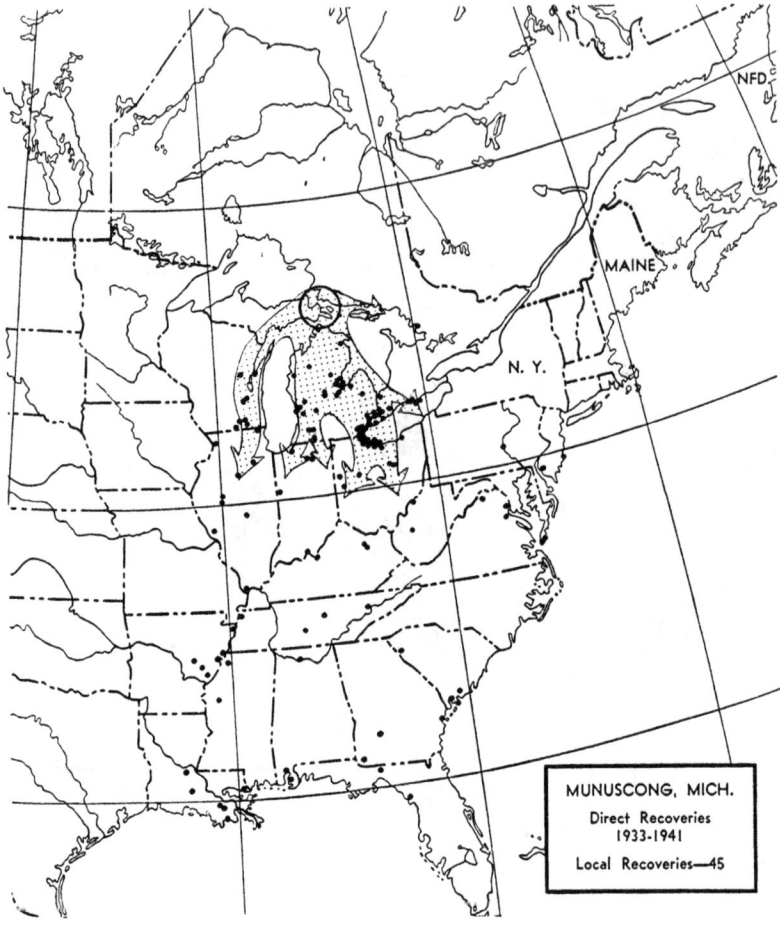

MUNUSCONG, MICH.

Direct Recoveries
1933-1941

Local Recoveries—45

Bibliography

1. ADDY, C. E.
Food Habits of the Black Duck on the Essex County Salt Marshes. Bull. Mass. Audubon Soc., February 1946.
2. ADDY, C. E., and L. G. MACNAMARA.
Waterfowl Management on Small Areas. Wildlife Management Institute, Washington, D. C. 1948.
3. ADDY, C. E.
Fall Migration of the Black Duck. Special Scientific Report: Wildlife No. 19, Fish & Wildlife Service, U. S. Department of the Interior, 1953.
4. ALDRICH, JOHN W., and others.
Migration of Some North American Waterfowl. A Progress Report on an analysis of banding records. Special Scientific Report (Wildlife) No. I. U. S. Fish & Wildlife Service, Washington, D. C. 1949.
5. ALLEN, C. S.
Hatching of the Black Duck. Proc. Lin. Soc., N. Y. #11. 1888.
6. . . . .
Nesting of the Black Duck on Plum Island, N. Y. Auk, Vol. 10, 1893.
7. AUSTIN, DR. OLIVER L.
Banding Records from Austin Station and Pleasant Bay. Unpublished Report.
8. BARRETT, S. A.
Ancient Aztalan, Bull. Pub. Mus. City of Milwaukee, Vol. XIII, pp. I–602.
9. BARTLETT, CHARLES O.
Some Waterfowl Observations in the Chochrane District of Northern Ontario—June-September, 1950. Unpublished Report. Dept. of Lands and Forests, Toronto, Ontario.
10. BEALL, H. W. and C. J. LOWE.
Forest Fires in New Brunswick, 1938-1946. Note 15.
Forest Fire Research, Forest Research Division, Forestry Branch, Department of Resources & Development, Ottawa, Ontario.
11. BELLROSE, FRANK C., and ELIZABETH BROWN CHASE.
Population Losses in the Mallard, Black Duck, and Blue-winged Teal. Biological Note No. 22, January 1950, Natural History Survey, Urbana, Illinois.

12. BENNETT, LOGAN J.
The Blue-Winged Teal, its Ecology and Management. Collegiate Press Inc., Ames, Iowa, 1938.
13. BENSON, DIRCK.
Studies in the Ecology of the Black Duck, *Anas rubripes Brewster*. Unpublished Thesis for the degree of Master of Arts. Cornell University, September 1937.
14. BENT, ARTHUR CLEVELAND.
Life Histories of North American Wildfowl, Order Anseres (part), 1923. U. S. Nat. Mus. Bull. 126.
15. BISSONETTE, THOMAS HUME.
Photoperiodicity in Birds. Wilson's Bull. Dec. 1937.
16. . . . .
Sexual Photoperiodicity. Journal of Heredity, Vol. XXVII. May, 1936.
17. BRADLEY, BEN O., and ARTHUR H. COOK.
Small Marsh Development in New York, Trans. 16th. N. A. Wildlife Conference, 1951, pp. 251.
18. BREWSTER, WILLIAM.
An Undescribed Form of Black Duck. Auk, Vol. 19, 1902.
19. BROLEY, JEANNE.
Identifying Nests of the Anatidae of the Canadian Prairies. Jour. Wildlife Mgt., Vol. 14, No. 4, Oct. 1950, pp. 452.
20. BURGER, J. WENDELL.
A Review of Experimental Investigations of Seasonal Reproduction in Birds. The Wilson Bull. Vol. 61, No. 4, Dec. 1949, pp. 411.
21. BURTCH, VERDI.
Nesting of the Black Duck in Yates County, New York. Auk, Vol. 27, 1910.
22. CARTWRIGHT, B. W.
Waterfowl Brood Counts in Manitoba, Saskatchewan, and Alberta, 1935, 1938-1942. Jour. Wildlife Mgt., Vol. 8, No. 1, Jan. 1944.
23. . . . .
Records of Black Ducks banded by Ducks Unlimited. Personal Correspondence, March 8, 1946.
24. CHRISTOFFERSON, K.
Common Black Duck, Red-legged Black Duck, and Mallard Sex Ratios. Bird Banding, Vol. 4, 1935.
25. CLARKE, C. H. D.
A Biological Investigation of the Thelon Game Sanctuary. Nat. Mus. of Canada. Bull. 96, Biological Series No. 25, Ottawa, 1940.
26. EATON, STEPHEN W.
Bird Distribution along the Peace, Slave, and Little Buffalo Rivers of Canada. Auk, Vol. 65, No. 3, July 1948.

27. EKLUND, CARL R. and LEON D. COOL.
Waterfowl Breeding Ground Survey in the Ungava Peninsula, Quebec, 1949. Special Scientific Report: Wildlife No. 2. U. S. Fish & Wildlife Service and Dominion Wildlife Service, Washington and Ottawa.

28. ELTON, CHARLES.
Voles, Mice and Lemmings. Oxford University Press, 1942.

29. EMMET, R. T.
Black Duck in Chihuahua. Auk, Vol. 5, 1888.

30. ERICKSON, ARNOLD B.
Sex-Ratios of Ducks in Minnesota, 1938-40. Auk, Vol. 60, No. 1, 1943.

31. FASSETT, NORMAN C.
The Vegetation of the Estuaries of Northeastern North America. Proc. Boston Soc. Nat. Hist. Vol. 39, No. 3, Nov. 1928.

32. FORBES, ALEXANDER.
Northernmost Labrador Mapped from the Air. American Geographical Society, New York, 1938.

33. FORBUSH, EDWARD HOWE.
Natural History of the Birds of Eastern and Central North America. Revised and abridged by John B. May 1939, Houghton Mifflin Co., Boston.

34. FREMONT, CHARLES.
La Grande Oie Blanche. Soc. Canadienne D'Histoire Naturelle, Bibliotheque des Jeunes Naturalistes, Tract 28, April, 1937.

35. FURNISS, O. C.
The Sex Ratio in Ducks. Wilson Bull., Dec. 1935.

36. GABRIELSON, IRA N., and BRUCE S. WRIGHT.
Notes on the Birds of Fort Chimo, Ungava District. Canadian Field-Naturalist, Vol. 65, No. 4, July-Aug. 1951.

37. GASHWILER, JAY S.
The Effect of Spring Muskrat Trapping on Waterfowl in Maine. Jour. Wildlife Mgt., Vol. 13, No. 2, April 1949.

38. GAUSE, G. F.
Struggle for Existence. Williams & Wilkins, Baltimore, 1934.

39. GENEROSOFF, V.
How to Increase the Wild Duck Supply. American Game, July, 1923.

40. GRENFELL, WILFRED T. and others.
Labrador. The Macmillan Co., New York, 1912.

41. GRIFFITH, R. E.
Black Ducks in Eastern Montana. Auk, Vol. 64, No. 3, 1947.

42. GRINNELL, JOSEPH.
The Black Duck in California. Condor, Vol. 13, 1911.

43. GRISCOM, LUDLOW.
An Ornithologist Looks at the Atlantic Flyway. Trans. 14th. N. A. Wildlife Conference 1949.

44. GROSS, ALFRED O.
The Black Duck Nesting in the Outer Coastal Islands of Maine. Auk, Vol. 62, No. 4, October 1945.

45. HAGAR, JOSEPH A.
Black Duck Bandings at the Austin Ornithological Research Station on Cape Cod, Mass. Bird Banding, Vol. XVII, No. 3, 1946, (Parts I & II), and (Part III), Vol. XVII, No. 4.

46. ....
Black Duck Mortality in the Parker River Region, Winter 1949-50. Report to Bureau of Wildlife Research and Management, Mass. Division of Fisheries and Game, Aug. 15, 1951.

47. HAMMOND, MERRILL C. and EDWARD J. SMITH, JR.
The Black Duck, *Anas rubripes*, in North Dakota. Auk, Vol. 67, No. 4, Oct. 1950.

48. HANSON, HAROLD C., MURRAY ROGERS and EDWARD S. ROGERS.
Waterfowl of the Forested Portions of the Canadian Pre-Cambrian Shield and the Palaeozoic Basin. Canadian Field-Naturalist, Vol. 63, No. 5, Sept.-Oct. 1949.

49. HAWKINS, ARTHUR S., and FRANK C. BELLROSE.
The Duck Flight and Kill Along the Illinois River During the Fall of 1938. American Wildlife. July-August 1939.

50. HEADSTROM, RICHARD.
Whose Nest is That? A guide to the bird nests found in Massachusetts. Mass. Audubon Society, 1944.

51. HERMAN, CARLTON M.
Contribution No. 25, Austin Ornithological Research Station. Jour. Parasitology, Vol. 24, No. 1, 1938.

52. HEWITT, OLIVER H.
The Bullfrog as a Predator on Ducklings. Jour. Wildlife Mgt., Vol. 14, No. 2, April 1950.

53. HICKEY, JOSEPH J.
A Guide to Bird Watching, Oxford University Press, 1943.

54. HILDEBRAND, HENRY.
Notes on the Birds of Ungava Bay District. Canadian Field-Naturalist, Vol. 64, No. 2, March-April, 1950.

55. HOCHBAUM, H. ALBERT.
The Canvasback on a Prairie Marsh. American Wildlife Institute, Washington, D. C., 1944.

56. ....
Recovery Potential in North American Waterfowl. Trans. 11th N. A. Wildlife Conference, 1946.

57. HOUSTON, C. STUART.
The Birds of Yorkton District, Saskatchewan. Canadian Field-Naturalist, Vol. 63, No. 6, Nov.-Dec. 1949.

58. Hunting and Fishing in Canada, October 1945.
59. HUSTICH, I.
The Phytogeographical Regions of Labrador. Arctic, Vol. 2,
No. 1, May 1949.
60. KORTWRIGHT, FRANCIS K.
The Ducks, Geese and Swans of North America. American
Wildlife Institute, Washington, D. C. 1943.
61. KUTZ, HARRY LEON.
The Diving Ability of the Black Duck. Jour. Wildlife Mgt.,
Vol. 4, No. 1, Jan. 1940.
62. LEOPOLD, ALDO.
Game Survey of the North Central States. Madison, Wisc.,
1931.
63. . . . .
Game Management. Charles Scribner's Sons, New York,
London, 1937.
64. . . . .
Lakes in Relation to Terrestial Life Patterns. Symposium
on Hydrobiology. University of Wisconsin Press, 1941.
65. LESHER, S. W. and S. C. KENDEIGH.
Effects of Photoperiod on Moulting of Feathers. Wilson Bull.
Sept. 1941.
66. LEWIS, HARRISON F.
Remarks on the Birds of Anticosti Island. Wilson Bull.,
June 1941.
67. . . . .
Destruction of Waterfowl by Oil. Wilson Bull., Sept. 1942.
68. LINCOLN, FREDERICK C.
Controlled Raising of Black Ducks.
American Game, May-June 1934.
69. . . . .
In Duck Shooting Along the Atlantic Tidewater. William
Morrow & Co., New York, 1947.
70. LOW, A. P.
Explorations in the Labrador. Report of the Geological
Survey of Canada, 1896.
71. LOW, JESSOP B.
Ecology and Management of the Redhead, *Nyroca americana*,
in Iowa. Ecological Monographs, 15: Jan. 1945.
72. LYNCH, JOHN J.
Marine Algae in Food of Rhode Island Waterfowl. Auk,
October 1939.
73. McCABE, ROBERT A.
The Homing of Transplanted Young Wood Ducks. Wilson
Bull. Vol. 59, No. 2, June, 1947.
74. MACFARLANE, R.
On an Expedition down the Begh-ula, or Anderson River.
Canadian Record of Science, Vol. IV, Jan. 1890.

75. MACOUN, JOHN.
Manitoba and the Great Northwest. The World Publishing
Company, Guelph, Ontario, 1882.

76. MANN, ROBERT.
Report of Banding Operations, 1943. McGinnes Slough, Or-
land Wildlife Refuge, Dictrict of Cook County, Ill.

77. MARTIN, A. C. and F. M. UHLER.
Food of Game Ducks in the United States and Canada. Tech-
nical Bull. No. 634, U. S. Dept. Agriculture. Washington,
D. C., March 1939.

78. McATEE, W. L.
Food Habits of the Mallard Ducks of the United States.
Bull. No. 720, U. S. Dept. of Agriculture. Washington, D. C.,
December 1918.

79. McCLANAHAN, ROBERT C.
Original and Present Breeding Ranges of Certain Game
Birds in the United States. Wildlife Leaflet BS-158, U. S.
Biological Survey. Washington, D. C., April 1940.

80. MENDALL, HOWARD L.
Food Habits in Relation to Black Duck Management in
Maine. Jour. Wildlife Mgt., Vol. 13, No. 1, Jan. 1949.

81. ....
Breeding Ground Improvements for Waterfowl in Maine.
Trans. 14th N. A. Wildlife Conference 1949.

82. ...., and JAY S. GASHWILER.
Green-Winged Teal Nesting in Maine. Auk, Vol. 58, 1941.

83. MUNRO, J. A.
The Northern Bald Eagle in British Columbia. Wilson Bull.,
March 1938.

84. MOUSLEY, HENRY.
Birth of a Black Duck Family. Auk, Oct. 1936.

85. NELSON, E. and JAY S. GASHWILER.
Blood Parasites of some Maine Waterfowl. Jour. Wildlife
Mgt., Vol. 5, No. 2, April 1941.

86. NICE, MARGARET MORSE.
Studies in the Life History of the Song Sparrow, Part I. A
Population Study of the Song Sparrow. Trans. Linnaen Soc.
of New York, Vol. IV, April 1937. and Part II. The Be
havior of the Song Sparrow and Other Passerines. Vol. VI,
Sept. 1943.

87. OLMSTEAD, ROGER O.
Feeding Habits of Great Horned Owls, *Bubo virginianus*.
Auk, Vol. 67, No. 4, Oct. 1950.

88. O'ROKE, EARL C.
A Malaria-like Disease of Ducks caused by *Leucocytozoon
anatis*, Wickware. University of Michigan School of Forestry
and Conservation. Bull. No. 4, 1934.

89. PERCY, LORD WILLIAM.
English Method of Restocking with Breeding Ducks. American Game. Feb., 1914.

90. PETERS, H. S.
Ring-Necked Duck Breeding in Prince Edward Island and Nova Scotia. Auk, July 1941.

91. ...., and THOMAS D. BURLEIGH.
The Birds of Newfoundland. Department of Natural Resources, Province of Newfoundland, St. John's, 1951.

92. PETRIDES, GEORGE A.
Sex Ratio in Ducks. Auk, 1944, pp. 565.

93. PHILLIPS, JOHN C.
Habits of the Two Black Ducks, *A. r. rubripes* and *A. r. tristis*. Auk, Vol. 37, 1920.

94. PHILLIPS, DR. JOHN C.
Is the Black Duck Extending its Range? American Game, Jan. 1922.

95. ...., and FREDERIC C. LINCOLN.
American Waterfowl. Houghton Mifflin Co., 1930.

96. ....
Eastern and Western Bred Waterfowl at Wenham, Mass. in the Past Thirty Years. Auk, Vol. XLIX, No. 4, Oct. 1932.

97. ....
Wenham Lake, Mass., Shooting Journal 1897-1935. Privately printed 1936 (?).

98. PIRNIE, MILES D.
Fall Migration of the Black Duck from Northern Michigan, Papers of the Michigan Academy of Science, Arts, and Letters, Vol. XV, 1931 (Published 1932).

99. ....
Michigan Waterfowl Management. Michigan Department of Conservation, Lansing, Mich., 1935.

100. POLUNIN, NICHOLAS.
Report on Botanical Explorations in Arctic America, 1946-1948. Arctic, Vol. 2, No. 1, May 1949.

101. PREBLE, EDWARD A.
North American Fauna No. 2. A Biological Investigation of the Athabasca-McKenzie Region. 1908.

102. PROVANCHER SOCIETY.
Annual Reports 1935-1944. Quebec, P. Q.

103. RANEY, EDWARD C.
Daily Movement of Young Black Duck. Auk, Jan. 1941.

104. RAYMOND, REV. WILLIAM O., LLD, F.R.S.C.
The River St. John, Reprinted by The Tribune Press, Sackville, N. B. 1943.

105. ROBINSON, L. LEWIS.
Eskimo Population in the Canadian Eastern Arctic. Canadian Geographical Journal. September, 1944.

106. ROGERS, STANLEY.
The Indian Ocean. George G. Harrap & Co. Ltd., London, Bombay and Sidney, 1932.

107. ROUSSEAU, JACQUES.
The Vegetation and Life Zones of George River, Eastern Ungava and the Welfare of the Natives. Arctic, Vol. 1, No. 2, 1948.

108. ROWAN, WILLIAM, D.Sc., F.R.S.C., F.Z.S.
Light and Seasonal Reproduction in Animals. Biological Review, Vol. 13, 1938.

109. SAWYER, EDMUND J.
The Courtship of Black Ducks. Bird Lore II: 195-196, 1909.

110. SAVILLE, D.B.O.
Bird Observations at Chesterfield Inlet, Keewatin, in 1950. Can. Field-Naturalist, Vol. 65, No. 4, July-Aug. 1951.

111. SHORTT, TERENCE M.
Correlation of Bill and Foot Coloring with Age and Season in the Black Duck. Wilson Bull. Vol. 55, No. 1, March 1943.

112. SNYDER, L. L.
Tradition in Bird Life. Canadian Field-Naturalist, Vol. 62, No. 2, March-April, 1949.

113. SOLMON, VICTOR E. F.
The Ecological Relation of Pike, *Esox lucius* L., and Waterfowl. Ecology, Vol. 26, No. 2, April 1945.

114. SOPER, J. DEWEY.
Ornithological Results of Baffin Island Expeditions of 1928-1929 and 1930-1931, together with more recent records. Auk, Jan. 1945.

115. SOWLS, LYLE K.
A Preliminary Report on Renesting in Waterfowl. Trans. 14th, N. A. Wildlife Conference, 1949, pp. 260.

116. STOUDT, JEROME H.
The Number of Waterfowl and the Kill on the Chippewa National Forest, 1937. Jour. Wildlife Mgt., July 1938.

117. TAVERNER, P. A.
Birds of Canada. Canadian Geological Survey, Nat. Mus. of Canada Bull. 72, Ottawa, 1934.

118. TINBERGEN, N.
The Function of Sexual Fighting in Birds: and the Problem of the Origin of "Territory." Bird Banding, Vol. VII, No. 1, Jan. 1936.

119. ....
The Behavior of the Snow Bunting in Spring. Trans. Linnaen Soc. of New York, Vol. V, Oct. 1939.

120. TODD, W. E. CLYDE.
The John B. Semple Expedition. The Cardinal, Vol. II, No. 1, Jan. 1927.

121. . . . .
The 1928 John B. Semple Expedition. Carnegie Magazine, Dec. 1928.

122. . . . .
A New Expedition to Hudson Bay. Carnegie Magazine, Feb. 1930.

123. . . . .
The 1930 Expedition to Hudson Bay. The Cardinal, Jan. 1931.

124. . . . .
A New Eastern Race of the Canada Goose. Auk, Vol. 55, Oct. 1938.

125. . . . .
More About Labrador. Carnegie Magazine. Dec. 1939.

126. . . . .
Birds of Western Pennsylvania, 1940.

127. . . . .
The Western Element of the James Bay Avifauna. Can. Field-Naturalist, April-May, 1943.

128. TOWNSEND, CHARLES W., M.D.
The Courtship of the Merganser, Mallard, Black Duck, Baldpate, Wood Duck and Bufflehead. Auk, Vol. 33, No. 1, Jan. 1916.

129. TRAUTMAN, MILTON B.
Ducks Following Bald Eagle. Wilson Bull., June 1942.

130. . . . .
Courtship Behavior of the Black Duck. Wilson Bull., Vol. 59, No. 1, March 1947.

131. TUCK, LESLIE M.
Occurrence of the Ring-Necked Duck in Newfoundland. Can. Field-Naturalist, Vol. 63, No. 5, Sept.-Oct. 1949.

132. TURNER, LUCIEN M.
List of the Birds of Labrador, Including Ungava, East Main, Moose, and the Gulf District of the Hudson's Bay Co., together with the Island of Anticosti. Proc. U. S. Nat. Mus., Vol. VIII, 1885.

133. VALIKANGAS, I.
Finnische Zugvogel aus englischen Vogeleiern. Vogelzug, 4: 159-166, 1933.

134. WILLIAMS, C. S. and WILLIAM H. MARSHALL.
Evaluation of Nesting Cover for Waterfowl on Bear River Refuge. Trans. N. A. Wildlife Conference 1938.

135. . . . . , et al.
Waterfowl Populations and Breeding Conditions—Summer 1948. Special Scientific Report 60. U.S. Fish & Wildlife Service & Dominion Wildlife Service. Washington, D. C., 1948.

136. ...., et al.
Waterfowl Populations and Breeding Conditions—Summer
1950. Special Scientific Report Wildlife No. 8. U. S. Fish and
Wildlife Service & Canadian Wildlife Service. Washington,
D. C., 1950.

137. WILLIAMS, C. S.
Atlantic Flyway Problems, Projects, and Prospects. Trans.
15th N. A. Wildlife Conference, 1950.

138. WITSCHI, EMIL.
Seasonal Sex Characters in Birds and their Hormonal Control. Wilson Bull., September 1935.

139. WRIGHT, BRUCE S.
Waterfowl Investigation in Eastern Canada, Newfoundland,
and Labrador, 1945-1947. Trans. 13th N. A. Wildlife Conference, 1948.

140. ....
Predation by the Eastern Chain Pickerel, *Esox niger,* on
Ducklings and Young Muskrats in the Estuary of the St.
John River. Unpublished Report to the National Research
Council, Ottawa, Ontario, 1949.

141. ....
The Relation of Bald Eagles to Breeding Ducks in New
Brunswick. Jour, Wildlife Mgt., Vol. 17, No. 1, Jan. 1953.

142. WRIGHT, HORACE W.
Black Duck Nesting in Boston Public Garden. Auk, Vol. 36,
1919.

Index

157